Praise for
Retirement Heaven or Hell

"A terrific book on a critical topic: your life in retirement.
Which, as I well know, can be God awful or terrific, depending
on *you*. Mike Drak is original, tough, and smart. A great guide
that cuts through a lot of nonsense and misunderstandings."
  —*Chris Crowley*, New York Times *Best-selling Author of the*
    Younger Next Year *Books*

"The topic of Mike's book is a really overlooked part of
retirement planning. Financial independence in retirement is
important, but money cannot buy happiness. The math part of
retirement is meaningless without addressing the emotional,
psychological, and spiritual parts of it. *Retirement Heaven or Hell*
is a refreshing read for retirees and aspiring retirees who are
striving for a fulfilling retirement."
  —*Jason Heath, CFP, Fee-only/Advice-only Financial Planner,*
    Objective Financial Partners

"Retirement should be a long, happy phase of life, and this book
tells you how you can make it that way. It's not only filled with
wisdom and inspiration, it's also an easy read and intensely
practical, in a way that anyone can implement. This is a book
you'll keep on your desk, not on your bookshelf."
  —*Don Ezra, Author of* Life Two *and Retirement Blogger*

"An important step toward enjoying a satisfying retirement is reading *Retirement Heaven or Hell*. This is a powerful blend of first-rate guidance and key questions to ask yourself to get the most out of this stage of life."

 —*Bob Lowry, Founder of Satisfying Retirement,*
  satisfyingretirement.blogspot.com

"Everyone needs to formulate their own retirement vision. This book tells you why this is so critically important and shows you how to create and follow the path you wish to take."

 —*Daryl Diamond, Author of the Best-seller* Your Retirement
  Income Blueprint *and* Retirement for the Record

"If you dream of early retirement or financial freedom, this book is for you. If you are nearing retirement but not sure how you will spend your time without work, this book is for you. If you are retired but getting bored and wondering if you should make a change, this book is for you. Following the advice in this book may add years to your life. More importantly it will add life to your years. Remember, 'There is no finish line.' Enjoy."

 —*Wealthy Doc, Physician Finance Blogger, WealthyDoc.Org*

"Mike Drak's new book shows a deep understanding of the challenges new retirees face. Not only does the book help readers to cope with life after retirement, it sets them on a quest to find meaning."

 —*Fred Vettese, Author of the Best-seller* Retirement Income
  for Life, The Essential Retirement Guide, *and*
  Co-author of The Real Retirement

"Wide is the path that leads to destruction in retirement, and narrow is the way that leads to life. Mike Drak and his co-authors have presented a candid and inspiring narrative that shows you how to make the most of your life in this place called retirement."

—*Mitch Anthony, Author of* The New Retirementality

"Life doesn't work like it used to. Increasing longevity is disrupting career paths, how we learn, and how we work. We need to explore alternative ways to adapt to the new normal, and this guide is a must-read for those navigating today's retirement reality."

—*Simon Chan, Vice President, Future of Work & Learning, Communitech*

"Is there such a place as Retirement Hell? Indeed, there is, and Mike Drak has experienced it firsthand. Fortunately for all of us, he survived the heat and has moved on to Retirement Heaven. In *Retirement Heaven or Hell*, he shares what he's learned during his journey for the benefit of all of us. This book is a must-read for those approaching retirement or those who have recently retired and found the transition more difficult than expected. It does an excellent job of working through the things that matter and the steps required to become a 'Retirement Rebel,' a title we should all strive to achieve."

—*Fritz Gilbert, Author of* Keys to a Successful Retirement *and Founder, TheRetirementManifesto.com*

RETIREMENT
HEAVEN OR HELL

RETIREMENT
HEAVEN OR HELL
Which Will You Choose?

9 Principles for Designing Your
Ideal Post-Career Lifestyle

MIKE DRAK
with SUSAN WILLIAMS and ROB MORRISON, CFP®

MILNER &
ASSOCIATES INC
· EDITING · PUBLISHING · COMMUNICATIONS · CONSULTING ·

ISBN 978-1-988344-30-0 (paperback)
ISBN 978-1-988344-31-7 (e-book)

Production Credits
Editor and project manager: Karen Milner
Copy editor: Lindsay Humphreys
Interior design and typesetting: Adrian So, AdrianSoDesign.com
Cover design: Adrian So, AdrianSoDesign.com
Printer: Friesens

Published by Milner & Associates Inc.
www.milnerassociates.ca

Printed in Canada
10 9 8 7 6 5 4 3 2 1

FSC
www.fsc.org
MIX
Paper from
responsible sources
FSC® C016245

This book is for people like us. People who believe that our third stage of life is filled with opportunity. People who believe we can contribute and make a difference as we age. People who are unwilling to settle for retirement mediocrity and want to live their later years with passion and purpose.

This book provides you with all you need to know to make this happen. It's now over to you to actually do it!

Contents

Foreword

by Ernie Zelinski

Someone once said, "Life begins when the kids move out and the cat gets run over." Today, for many people, that is when they reach so-called "retirement age." Each time of life has special challenges where most of us can use some special guidance, and this is certainly one of them.

Much has been said about retirement in the last few decades, both positive and negative. Nowadays some people hate the word; others are comfortable with it. I am fine with the term because to me it doesn't mean disengagement from both work and life, like it means to others.

The purpose of this book is to help the retired and the soon-to-be retired better understand their lifetime aspirations, to help them minimize the complexity and uncertainty associated with retirement, and to allow them to concentrate on what matters most in retirement planning. As the author of three different retirement-related books, I should know a bit about this phase of life and how to handle it with ease. Nevertheless, I learned a lot from Mike's book, and you will too if you keep an open mind.

An end to full-time work is great, but only if you know what you enjoy, how you will spend your days, and what your ideal lifestyle will cost. For this you must have some sort of plan. So, what is your retirement plan?

In one strip of Scott Adams's Dilbert cartoon, Wally responds to Dilbert's declaration that a study shows most people don't have any kind of retirement plan by saying, "I plan to live an unhealthy lifestyle and pass away in my cubicle, preferably on a Monday." Dilbert replies, "That's a terrible plan." Wally quips, "Better than average, according to you."

I hope you have devised a much better than average retirement plan. That's what it takes to have a happy, heavenly retirement. Of course, retirement planning isn't only about the money; retirement should be joyful in all regards. Mike emphasizes that you don't need a lot of money to enjoy a great retirement; you just need to know what's important to you and be resourceful with the amount of money you have.

To be sure, happiness in retirement is a personal thing. What will make you feel fulfilled is completely different from what others will find rewarding. Nevertheless, there are certain traits and behaviors common to those who experience a happy retirement, and Mike unlocks the secrets to Retirement Heaven by revealing the nine most important principles to follow.

He emphasizes that "You need to find balance and the right retirement mix of work, leisure, health, and relationships" in order to have a happy retirement. Put another way, in this phase of life we all have instruments that we must treat with great care if we are to experience Retirement Heaven instead of Retirement Hell. The instruments are our bodies, our minds, our spirits, and our financial resources. As Mike further states, "If not managed properly, retirement can be a living hell."

Will the final phase of your life be heavenly or hellish? It's your call, according to Mike, and the outcome is in your control. Retirement Hell is not a pleasant place to be. To be sure, you don't want to spend the last years of your life bored or anxious, or simply marking time and waiting for the end. On the other hand, this can be the best time of your life if you create your own Retirement Heaven through proper planning and self-awareness.

The way I see it, you will have attained true freedom in this world when you can get up in the morning when you want to get up; go to sleep when you want to go to sleep; and in the interval, work and play at the things you want to work and play at—all at your own pace. The great news is that retirement allows you the opportunity to attain a new sense of purpose and freedom. Mike Drak masterfully opens us to that possibility.

Ernie J. Zelinski
International Best-Selling Author and
Unconventional Career Coach

Author of the bestseller *How to Retire Happy, Wild, and Free* (over 400,000 copies sold and published in nine foreign languages) and the international bestseller *The Joy of Not Working* (over 310,000 copies sold and published in seventeen foreign languages)

Introduction

Retirement: Less an Ending, More a New Start

L ike most people, I thought retiring would be easy; however, for me, it was anything but, especially after being pushed out of the only company I had ever worked for after thirty-six years. I struggled early on, trying to figure things out. Looking for answers, I read every book on the subject of retirement that I could get my hands on but was disappointed, as most were focused on the financial planning aspect of retirement. None of the books went to the heart of the matter and gave me the answers I was looking for. Namely, what would make me happy and, more importantly, what was I going to do with the rest of my life?

After working hard throughout my career—saving for and dreaming of the end goal of retirement—now that I was suddenly there, it was nothing like I'd imagined it would be. I felt lost and aimless, well on the way to spiraling down into Retirement Hell.

When the Student Is Ready, the Teacher Appears

This well-known Buddhist saying suggests that there is a certain order to the universe and things will happen when they are

supposed to. But for them to happen, the student needs to be ready for change and have the mind-set to receive it. Believe me, at that point in my life, at the crossroads of retirement, I was more than ready; I just needed someone to show me the way.

Then one day I attended a seminar where Seth Godin was the keynote speaker and each attendee was given his book *What to Do When It's Your Turn (and It's Always Your Turn)*. That title haunted me for a long time, and the seminar turned out to be one of my biggest "aha" moments, when everything started to make sense and I suddenly knew exactly what I needed to do from that point forward. It felt like Seth was personally challenging me to take action so that I could achieve the lasting happiness I was after. He was telling me that it was now up to me to gain control of my future and achieve the life that I had always wanted. I had paid my dues, and because of that I had earned a turn to do whatever I wanted with my new-found freedom.

Reading Seth's book helped pull me out of Retirement Hell and set me on a path to figure out who I really was and what I wanted to become. I realized that retirement wasn't the end goal I'd been striving for but, rather, a new beginning; a chance to design and live the rest of my life on my own terms.

Thinking about the question posed in Seth's book (What are you going to do when it's your turn?) excited and terrified me. It was essentially the same question I was asked when I was much younger: "What do you want to do with the rest of your life?"

I was never able to answer that question as a child, and even when I finished school, I still didn't know what I wanted to do. I had no idea about what I would be good at; I just basically fell into the first job I was offered and stayed there for the next thirty-six years of my life. I was now being given a second chance to answer that same question and I wanted to be able to give a good answer this time.

The easy answer for most people is to just say they want to retire because they're tired of working and the daily grind. Many crave a permanent vacation because this is what the advertisers have convinced us would make us happy. But really, when you think about it, what exactly would you be retiring *to*?

It's foolhardy to blindly follow conventional expectations and expect to enjoy a great retirement, because the truth is that it's hard to enjoy retirement when you are not doing what *you* like to do. Living someone else's retirement dream is a sure ticket to Retirement Hell. To define your own Retirement Heaven, you first have to throw out the idea of traditional retirement as the end of something, and do some heavy soul-searching and planning to design a life beyond your working years that you'll be happy living.

What did I now want to do with the rest of my life? It took a lot of self-reflection before I was finally able to answer that question for myself, but what I did know right out of the gate was that I didn't want to waste my turn and just retire in the traditional way like everyone else.

Victory Lap Retirement: Discovering Your Special Mission

My quest to get out of Retirement Hell and find my own little piece of heaven here on earth in my new post-career life ultimately led to me co-writing my first book, *Victory Lap Retirement*. It challenges the idea of traditional full-stop retirement and rejects the notion of retirement as an end goal in and of itself. Victory Lap is our version of a better mousetrap—a way to stay healthier, more active, and more engaged in what could be the longest and most fulfilling phase of your life. The fact is, people are living longer than ever before, so you have to find new ways of making your retirement not only financially sustainable but also vibrant and stimulating, possibly for two or three decades—maybe even longer than your career years.

Although you will see the word "retirement" used throughout this book, because that is what people are used to hearing, creating your own Victory Lap is really what you should be striving for. Your Victory Lap is all about designing a retirement lifestyle that is unique to you, based on your own needs and values, not on someone else's vision of what retirement should be. It starts with discovering your special mission in life—or rediscovering it if you put it on the back burner in your working years while you took care of business, your family, and other people's priorities rather than your own.

Since the release of *Victory Lap Retirement*, I've spent a lot of time doing more research, talking to retirees and hearing their stories, and doing a great deal of self-reflection. These efforts have resulted in me developing some new insights and beliefs about retirement and why it is that many people (myself included) have a hard time transitioning, as well as how that journey can be made easier (which is the whole point of this book).

This may sound weird to some of you, but I believe we are all part of some kind of giant master plan and that each of us was created for a reason. Call it God's plan, the universe, the Force, or whatever power you believe in that's greater than any of us. I am convinced that each of us has been given unique skills, abilities, and a special mission that needs to be fulfilled; and until we find out what that special purpose is and start working on it, we will never feel complete.

> The two most important days in your life are the day you are born and the day you find out why.
> —Mark Twain

I believe that each of us can discover the unique mission we are born to fulfill by identifying our "innate needs" that serve as a sort of GPS to guide us through life. Unlike personal values that we develop over time and that can change as we evolve, these needs are always there. It's like a hunger inside us that needs to be fed or we will never feel satisfied. This hunger will be stronger in some and weaker in others, but we all experience innate needs to some degree.

We are all hardwired with a need for "significance": the need for achievement, accomplishment, contribution, connection, and autonomy. And we have an inborn need to feel valued, both by ourselves and by others. If we don't find a way to feed our innate needs through completion of our mission, the hunger will never go away. It will keep gnawing at us until we find a way to satisfy it.

Many retirees feel this hunger, a kind of emptiness, after the initial honeymoon period of no longer working. Despite having their material needs met, they feel lost and a sense that something is missing, because their work was the source of nourishment for their innate needs. Until they find another way of feeding their innate needs, they are never going to be genuinely happy.

Some people whose hunger is not that strong will be able to ignore the uneasiness and just choose to get by and settle for what happens. Others will try to numb the feeling with self-medicating: eating too much, drinking too much, or vegging in front of the TV trying to make the feeling go away. But it never does.

And if you think that having a lot of money will cure things, it won't. I know a lot of people who have a lot of money yet are miserable in retirement. They are unhappy because they feel unfulfilled, and this feeling will persist until they find a way of satisfying their innate needs and completing their mission. Don't believe me? Take a look at what is happening in the FIRE community.

Everyone is talking about the FIRE movement these days, whereby the goal is to gain Financial Independence and Retire Early, but all the people I know that have achieved FIRE are still working in some capacity. For some reason, many of them feel the need to deny that they are still working, but why deny the truth? The lesson here is that even when you become financially independent and get your freedom back, you still need to find interesting, rewarding things to fill your day with, and working at something you enjoy is one of the best ways of doing that. FIRE is still a good concept, one that I'm teaching my kids; they just need to redefine the RE part.

Why do you think the Rolling Stones keep performing? They have more money than they will ever spend, but performing, feeling appreciated, and seeing how good they make people feel satisfies their innate needs. It's what drives Mick Jagger and keeps him not just alive but thriving in his seventies. I hate to see what will happen to the band when they can't tour anymore.

Why would you ever retire from something you love to do that makes you feel good about yourself? It just doesn't make sense to me. Keep in mind, "work" in your Victory Lap doesn't have to mean the same thing as it did during your full-time working life. The key at this stage is to find something truly meaningful to you to keep active and engaged—not just to occupy your time or supplement your income, but to fulfill your innate needs, your purpose. Pursuing your mission in Victory Lap might mean being paid for the work you choose to do, or it might not. The point is to work at something or toward something because you want to, not because you have to.

Retirement success is not about sitting around and taking it easy for the rest of your life. It's about completing your mission and finding significance and connectedness through what you can give. It's about finding fulfillment through some purposeful activity—whatever that means to you.

My Mission

I always felt that there was something special I was meant to do, but I wasn't always doing it throughout my primary career while working for the Corp (short for the corporation). Looking back, I realize that I always found meaning and fulfillment in helping others, and I lost that outlet when I lost my job. I've also realized that in my struggle to get out of Retirement Hell, I was unknowingly being prepared through firsthand experience so that others could benefit from what I had learned.

My retirement transition was all trial and error and it was painful and frustrating, but it doesn't have to be that way for you. Think of me as a retirement crash test dummy. I've spent a lot of time figuring things out and so, by sharing what I've learned, I can shorten your learning curve and help make your retirement journey a lot less hazardous and painful. My mission is to share my personal story, my mistakes made, and my lessons learned to help you make the same transition, but without all the stress, fear, and worry about what's next that I went through.

This book contains everything I've learned about retirement and how we can live longer, healthier, happier lives. It's a book about possibility, finding purpose, and having fun in retirement. I felt the need to write it because the conventional retirement story they like to tell us no longer works today. It's a big mistake to live a retirement devoid of accomplishment, success, and failures. We were not born to merely survive and then retire, full stop. Once we've left our primary career behind, we need to continue to matter, to make a difference, to contribute, to help the world be a better place. And, believe me, the world needs a lot of help right now.

Forced retirement was my wake-up call to start living life on my terms. After a short trip through Retirement Hell (but not short enough), today I'm healthier, happier, and more grateful than I've ever been. I've reconnected with my family and friends and I'm feeling pretty good about myself. I no longer feel the need to compete, compare, or worry about what others think. I don't care about those things anymore. I have fully arrived in Retirement Heaven.

I'm sharing my personal story throughout this book so you can learn the fundamental truths that will help you get what you want out of your own Victory Lap and lead you to a heavenly retirement that's perfect for you—one that is aligned with your needs, interests, and goals. It is within your grasp, but it will take some work to figure out what that will look like.

What Does Retirement Heaven Look Like?

Unfortunately, I can't answer that question for you because everyone's mission, values, and retirement journey are different. However, what I have learned from my research is that retired people basically fall into two broad categories: comfort-oriented retirees and growth-oriented retirees.

Comfort-oriented retirees like to have a safe, ordinary retirement. They enjoy being comfortable and are often unwilling to risk becoming uncomfortable. These are the people who are content with conventional full-stop retirement. The majority have saved enough money to support a modest retirement, and some of them have been fortunate enough to accumulate a great deal of money. They don't want to work; in fact, they don't want to do much of anything that will take them out of their comfort zone. These type of folks probably would never spend the time to read a book like this because they are content just the way they are.

Happiness levels for people in this group often plateau. They are usually quite happy with the way things are and comfortable living in a very predictable way. These people have chosen a life of certainty, and as a result they become uninterested in trying new things. Their life never changes. They no longer have any goals; retiring was their biggest goal, and now that it's behind them, they avoid things that will stretch or test them.

My mother was a comfort-oriented retiree. She lived a simple life and was content to spend all of her days helping her family, taking care of her cat, and enjoying time with her friends. That was what made her happy. She never felt the need to go out and run a marathon or travel the world. She was content with the simple things and spending time with friends and family. My mother showed me that you don't need much in order to be happy. Just the basics: food on the table, a roof over your head, and some level of financial security. When you have these things, there isn't much to complain about.

Living like that isn't wrong—it's just wrong for people like me, the growth-oriented retirees. Unlike the comfort-oriented retirees, we refuse to take our foot off the gas and become complacent, because we know that continually setting new goals and realizing our retirement potential will make us happier.

Growth-oriented retirees are the "retirement rebels"—the people who have a strong inner voice constantly telling them to never be satisfied; to keep stretching, exploring, learning, and experiencing. They are the retirees who have created a bucket list a mile long and plan on knocking things off that list for as long as they can. Every goal they achieve gives them a "happiness hit" and a feeling of achievement and satisfaction. But they know this feeling will be short-lived, so they continually establish new goals and start working on them to get the next happiness hit.

At the end of the day, though, it doesn't matter which group you belong to, as long as you are happy and doing things that are meaningful and fulfilling to *you*. And that's our primary reason for writing this book—to help you figure out what it is you truly want out of retirement, because only you can determine what will be Retirement Heaven for you. The book is intended as a companion to *Victory Lap Retirement* (co-written by Rob, me, and Jonathan Chevreau), but it can be used on its own. The whole point is not only to read this book, but to work through it—to wrestle with the ideas and the soul-searching questions it contains to design your very own Victory Lap.

The book is organized into four main sections: Part 1 outlines the retirement transition process in detail and describes what you will experience as you transition through the various stages. Part 2 introduces the nine retirement principles that are key for enjoying a successful retirement. Part 3 deals with the important search for purpose, looking for clues from your past to identify your core values, the things that when satisfied will make you happy; and introduces the idea of finding meaningful work if you decide you want that as part of an active, vibrant Victory Lap. Part 4 introduces the concept of retirement lifestyle design and the importance of establishing value-based goals based on the retirement principles.

At the end of each chapter, there are simple but powerful questions that will help create breakthroughs, if you are willing to go deep within yourself and provide completely honest answers. Some of the questions might make you feel uncomfortable, but those are the most important ones to answer if you want to enjoy a great retirement.

We recommend that you read this guide in its entirety before officially starting to implement the principles and exercises. This will give you a big-picture feel for what you will be working toward, and then you can go back and put the ideas into practice. That said, this book was written to be useful to as many retirees as possible: for people who have a lot of money as well as people who do not have as much. For that reason, not everything in this book will be a good fit for you, and that's OK. Just take the parts that work for you and ignore the rest.

As you go through the book, you will become more positive about your retirement and what is possible for you. As you start work on designing your new lifestyle, you will find your attitude improving as you become aware of, and motivated by, the possibilities that lie ahead of you. Your vision for the future will make you excited, which will give you increased energy and belief in what you plan on doing.

Retirement should be the payoff for all your hard work, not a stage in your life that is simply endured. We don't want you to just exist and get by; we want you to push past your perceived limitations of what's possible and find new purpose that will make you want to jump out of bed in the morning. We want you to be able to live financially stress-free, maintain good health, and spend quality time with your family and friends, making as many wonderful memories as you can—because, at the end of the day, that is all that you are going to be left with.

Instead of viewing retirement as a finish line, look at it as a starting point, the first day of the rest of your life. A time when you finally get to do things that are meaningful and matter—the things that you love to do. Best to think of it this way: Traditional retirement is an end. Victory Lap is a new beginning. It's your opportunity to live the life you always dreamed about because it's all about you now. Most of your major financial obligations are behind you at this stage and, therefore, you have an opportunity to do things differently, to do things that you want to do but never had a chance to pursue until now. So, don't limit yourself. Our hope for you is that you have the Retirement Heaven of your dreams!

LESSONS FROM A PANDEMIC

As I was putting the finishing touches on the manuscript for this book, the COVID-19 pandemic hit. I started experiencing a ringing in my ears due to my high blood pressure; it was spiking with my increased anxiety about the coronavirus and my feeling incredibly lost and vulnerable. It suddenly hit me that I had felt these same feelings before, when I was kicked out of my thirty-six-year banking career. But it wasn't Sudden Retirement Shock this time; it was COVID-19 shock, brought on by a traumatic world event that changed the life of every individual person. We were all in uncharted territory and literally scared for our lives and what the future might bring. At the end of the day, the feelings are similar in the case of both types of shock.

I felt the need to go back to my finished manuscript and include some reflections on how people felt during the pandemic, and how these feelings mirror what people experience during retirement transition. You will find these observations and comments in boxes sprinkled throughout the book. I hope you find these "Lessons from a Pandemic" to be as eye-opening as I did.

The self-isolation during COVID-19 gave many people approaching retirement age a glimpse of what retirement might feel like—an abrupt end to work, loss of social connection and trying to make ends meet on a much lower income—and many people weren't very happy with the experience. Think of the pandemic and what you went through as a trial run, a test case that opened your eyes to the real retirement you will be facing better than any financial plan ever could.

How successfully you dealt with the COVID-19 lockdown might give you a good indication of how successful you will be in retirement if you don't plan ahead for this very different phase of life. No matter what your experience was like of life during the pandemic, this book will help you use it to help prepare for life after work.

PART 1

PREPARE YOURSELF FOR RETIREMENT

1

The Big Retirement Dip

Be Careful What You Wish For

It's not stress that kills us, it's our reaction to it.
—Hans Selye

As we approach our retirement years, our stress level can increase substantially due to too many life changes occurring in a short period of time, followed by high stress associated with the actual transition to retirement. Some of us are stressed because our kids are living in our basement, burdened by high levels of student debt and unable to find a good-paying job. Some of us are stressed because our parents are aging and need our help. Some of us are stressed by the possibility of losing our job and not being able to find another one that pays as well. Some of us are stressed over not having saved enough money for retirement, and some of us are stressed by all of the above.

Some people think they can reduce stress in their lives by no longer working, so they end up following the traditional full-stop retirement route and allow themselves to be put out to pasture.

They have accepted the view of retirement as being a finish line—a line that, once crossed, means they don't have to work anymore. They believe that they can just relax and live happily ever after. They expect that their life will suddenly become wonderful and all their problems will disappear because they no longer have to work.

The truth is that retiring (or being forced to retire) only to play golf, walk the malls, and waste countless hours watching reruns on TV will not reduce stress but, in fact, will increase it further. You will be stressed by the loss of purpose, loss of structure, loss of routine, loss of work friends, loss of a sense of accomplishment, loss of employment income, and a loss of identity. To top it off, you may be further stressed over your declining health caused by all the stress you are experiencing. How sad is that?

This stage of your life is full of enormous changes, and lots of them, and it's not unusual to feel anxious and overwhelmed as a result. Because most people haven't been exposed to such high levels of emotional stress before, they haven't developed the necessary resiliency to recover quickly and bounce back. They start to become pessimistic, and it's hard to be resilient when you've lost hope for the future. Trying to cope with it all, more than a few retirees start to break out the wine before five o'clock, and knowing that this is the wrong thing to do only increases their hopelessness. Welcome to Retirement Hell!

The Three Stages of Life After Work

Full-stop retirement may not be the fun, relaxing ride you thought it would be. This can be not only disappointing but downright anxiety-provoking, and it can give you that same sick feeling in your stomach that you get from riding a roller coaster. Although you may not have expected retirement to feel like this, your reaction to such an abrupt major change in your life does often follow predictable stages: In the beginning the ride is pleasant, starting off on a slow, steady incline. The view looks quite nice and things are feeling pretty good—until you hit the sudden drop straight into Retirement Hell. From there, you experience many twists and turns that seem never ending. When you think the ride is about to end, suddenly you get hit by another curve. Thankfully, at some point things start to settle down and you start the long uphill climb out of Retirement Hell.

It's important to recognize that not everyone's ride will be of the same intensity. Some people really love roller coasters, but when it comes to your future, do you want to risk having a ride that is stressful and out of your control? People who experience the scarier ride are the ones who, like me, were pushed out of their job or who enjoyed their work and identified too much with it and have a hard time letting go. When the choice of when to retire is taken away from us (that is, made for us), the ride through Retirement Hell will be scarier and longer. Take it from someone who knows.

Figure 1.1 illustrates what the typical retirement journey looks like for someone who is disappointed to find out that full-stop retirement isn't all it's cracked up to be. You can and will get through it, but it can be a wild ride.

Figure 1.1: The Big Retirement Dip

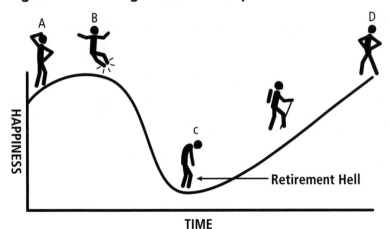

Having a good understanding of what you are about to go through in transitioning to traditional retirement makes the ride much easier to get through. When you know what is coming your way, you can prepare for it and you won't be surprised by what you are experiencing. With that in mind, let's break down the retirement ride into its three main stages.

After spending years working for a living, people are tired, and the thought of retiring and living a life of leisure as portrayed by the advertisers and society in general is pretty appealing: no more work, no more getting up early to make a long commute, no more being told what to do, no more structure or routines to follow, you are free to do what you want when you want.

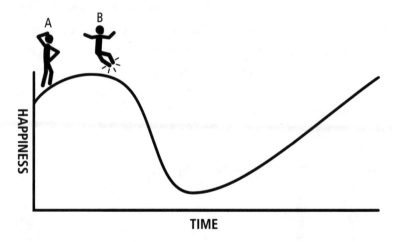

Stage One: The Honeymoon Stage

You can sleep in or travel to all those places you used to dream about. You can golf as much as you like or spend lots of time with the grandkids. People in this stage start knocking things off their to-do lists, doing all the things they never had time to do while they were working; things like making repairs around the house, gardening, or painting. It feels great to get things accomplished and be as free as a bird. This feeling of retirement bliss generally lasts up to a year before the new reality sinks in.

Once they have completed everything on their list, growth-oriented retirees often find that they need to find something else to do, and this is when the trouble starts. Without a bigger plan or a purpose, they start to slide down to Retirement Hell, the lowest point in the Big Retirement Dip. Although a life of leisure can be rejuvenating for a little while, even for growth-oriented retirees, at some point they get a sense that the party is over. They start to get a little antsy and begin looking for something more interesting and challenging to do. Or they fall into a state of general malaise and emptiness without the source of satisfaction and accomplishment that they used to get from their work.

Interestingly, some comfort-oriented retirees will be able to remain happily in the Honeymoon Stage for their entire retirement, even though they might seem to have less meaning in their lives compared with growth-oriented retirees. They don't need much in order to be content: food, clothes, and a roof over their head works for them. They are happy that they don't have to work again (they never did like that part), and they don't care or worry much about anything. They avoid doing anything challenging and are free to sleep in and live a life of leisure. They don't even care what day it is because every day to them is a holiday. The simple life is exactly what they want, and they feel good living like that. All I can say is, different strokes for different folks. Who am I to judge?

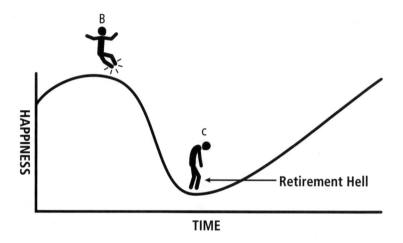

Stage Two: The Party's Over:
Welcome to Retirement Hell

Even if you enjoy a blissful honeymoon period of freedom immediately after you stop working, being unprepared for retirement often leads to Sudden Retirement Shock, a feeling of being incredibly lost and vulnerable, which is Retirement Hell at its worst. Your heart isn't into hobbies and activities that used to bring you joy, and you begin to wonder if that's all there is. Suddenly, the life of leisure you dreamed about for so long and even enjoyed for a while becomes empty and meaningless.

If you can't find a way to manage your retirement shock, depression will eventually set in, and depression is a very bad thing. It robs you of your energy, vitality, and self-esteem. With depression typically comes an unrelenting sad mood; it's harder to focus and harder to feel inspired or care about anything. You feel like you are just going through the motions.

When you are in the deepest depths of Retirement Hell and suffering from Sudden Retirement Shock, even easy things such as having to fix a clogged toilet become hard and feel like huge problems. You may have difficulties sleeping and eating. At a seminar we gave in Chicago, a woman who had recently lost her husband said that the Big Retirement Dip was very similar to the five stages of grief. She's right, because in retirement it's not uncommon to experience loss—the loss of both structure and of our identity.

It's hard to find help for Sudden Retirement Shock because most of the people in your life (especially your spouse if he or she is still working) can't seem to understand what you are going through. They can't relate to you being unhappy because you don't have to go to work anymore. It just doesn't make sense to them.

LESSONS FROM A PANDEMIC

We could easily change the name of this chapter from "The Big Retirement Dip" to "The Big Pandemic Dip" because the experience is the same. We all suffered from COVID-19 shock when our lives were suddenly turned upside down. Sure, it might have felt good for the first couple of days of the lockdown, not having to set an alarm, not having to deal with a terrible commute, and not having a demanding work schedule that left us exhausted most evenings. Initially, the freedom we gained was very liberating; but it wasn't long till reality sank in and most of us found ourselves in pandemic hell.

In retirement, we grieve the loss of our work and the sense of identity and social connection we used to have because of it. During the COVID-19 pandemic, many people in mid-career felt the same loss of their "normal" lives, their financial security, their social groups, and even loss of work itself.

If you lost your work and along with it your daily structure, routines, and purpose during the pandemic, what did you do? What got you out of bed in the morning?

Because people can't empathize with your situation, you give up trying to make them understand and instead you look for ways to dull your pain. Drinking too much, eating too much, shopping too much, or becoming somewhat of a recluse are common escapes. Living like this, though, for a prolonged period, will make the situation far worse and could be dangerous to your health (more about that later).

This is something you want to nip in the bud before things get out of hand. It is best to talk to someone who understands and has already gone through what you are currently experiencing. The services of a retirement coach might help here, but only when you are ready to listen and take action. This book can help you get into the right mind-set, and it may even help to coach you through this difficult stage.

People Who Will Have a Harder Time Transitioning

People whose life was their work will find moving on from their primary career the most difficult. It's incredibly disheartening for them to wake up to the fact that because of their devotion to their career, other than the money and some trinkets they earned along the way, their prize is a strained relationship with their spouse and family and few real friends. Things weren't supposed to work out this way, were they?

It's natural to be angry also if your exit came sooner than expected and/or it was handled poorly, as happened in my case. When you were a loyal soldier, it just doesn't feel right to be treated like that after so many years of personal sacrifice and commitment; to be banished from your tribe and sent out into the wasteland. Without our tribe we lose our identity, our purpose, and our feeling of safety. On the positive side, though—and there is always a positive side—you need to see getting kicked out of your work tribe for the opportunity that it really is. Losing your job gives you a chance to find something better.

Following are some stories about recent retirees I have observed in my own neighborhood during my daily walks. It's possible that they're happy with their current lifestyle, but my guess is they'll soon be in Retirement Hell, if they're not there already.

Window Guy

Window Guy and his wife both retired at the same time. I don't see her much, as she spends most of her time in their house doing whatever, and Window Guy spends most of his time outside doing yard maintenance and washing things: their cars, the siding on their house, the windows. I knew he was really hurting when I noticed him more than once washing his lawnmower and snowblower. Guys like Window Guy usually crack in the winter when they can't wash anything; that's when they get stressed out and end up making some bad decisions.

Window Guy and his wife didn't have a lot of friends, and in the spring he told me they had decided to downsize and move to a small town just like they suggest in some of the retirement books, so that they could put some more money into their retirement accounts. I don't think they needed the extra money because they didn't seem to go anywhere. I don't know how it worked out for them, but I'm concerned because they didn't have many friends before and I don't think they will be making many new friends in that new town of theirs either.

Weed Woman

I really don't know Weed Woman other than to say hi when I walk by her house. She is somewhat similar to Window Guy except she spends most of her day pulling weeds out in her front yard. I think she does it as her way of socializing. I'm not sure if she lives alone, but I've never seen anyone with her. Again, I always wonder what people like Weed Woman and Window Guy do in the winter.

RV Man

RV Man lives a couple of streets over from me and is married. He was an accountant, and when he retired he bought an RV to use when he and his wife go to Florida each winter. What intrigues me is that he seems to have developed a new life since buying that RV. He spends most of his time in it in the summer watching TV, and his wife spends most of her time in the house. It's as if they have two separate homes. I wouldn't be surprised if he sleeps there as well, he loves that RV so much. Retirement sure makes some people do some strange things, and it will be interesting to see how things turn out for those two.

I worry about people like Window Guy, Weed Woman, and RV Man, and there are a lot of retirees just like them. They are struggling with the loss of structure and routine that their work gave them, trying to find ways to utilize all the free time they now have on their hands. If they have a partner who is also retired, they don't know how to adjust to the increased togetherness, and it's causing both them and their partners a great deal of stress.

When winter hits, people like Window Guy and Weed Woman start to feel a lack of purpose even more keenly. They can't wash windows or pick weeds anymore and they become anxious, frustrated, bored, angry, and confused. Most days, they feel like they are drifting in a fog and they can't find a way out. They know they need to make some changes in their retirement, and so they start to think about things, and that's when the fear and frustration sink in. They are scared about not having enough money for retirement; they are scared about losing their health; they are scared that their spouses and kids might not love them anymore; and they are frustrated by not having anything fulfilling to do.

The negative stereotyping of older adults bothers them. They are expected to take it easy, play it safe, and start to wind down—get involved in social and recreational activities like playing shuffleboard. But they are not ready to live like that. That's for old people, and they are not there yet. They still have a need to achieve and matter, but unfortunately, they don't have a plan nor do they know what to do, and that is why the depression takes hold.

Some people, the lucky ones, will be able to get out of Retirement Hell quickly after a period of boredom and frustration. They'll spend time exploring their options and questioning things until they come up with a solution for themselves. Others will stay much longer, lost in their feelings and emotions, continuing to live in the past and feel sorry for themselves. They may even decide to just accept things as they are, become complacent, and settle in for the duration. They don't know what they want to do or where they want to go, so they just default to doing nothing and feeling sorry for themselves for the rest of their lives.

Men generally have a harder time dealing with retirement transition and can waste years lost in Retirement Hell, watching TV and living in denial rather than actively facing their future and trying to figure things out.

Anyone trapped in Retirement Hell feels like their head is spinning and filled with questions such as:

- Who am I?
- Why is my partner always mad at me?
- Why don't my kids want to spend more time with me?
- Where did all my friends go?
- What am I going to do with the rest of my life?
- Why do I feel like this?
- Is this all there is for me?
- What am I here for?

People stuck at the bottom of the Big Retirement Dip have a hard time restarting and begin to withdraw, isolating themselves from others. They feel alone even when they are surrounded by their closest friends. They struggle with letting go of their past familiar life and carry a lot of emotional baggage in the form of grudges, anxiety, depression, and other negative feelings. They feel like a failure; they're defeated; they've hit rock bottom—and knowing that depresses them because retirement wasn't supposed to be like this.

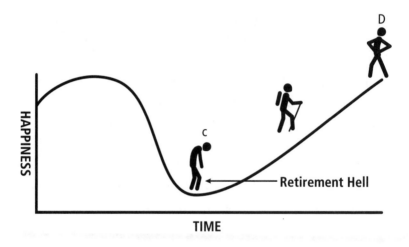

Stage Three: Escaping from Retirement Hell

It's hard to fix things when you are in a bad mood and have no energy. When you're tired and frustrated, everything feels difficult and everything bothers you. You just want to be left alone with your negative thoughts so you can try and find a way out of the mess you're in, but it's next to impossible to improve things when you feel like that.

So, how can you create momentum? By committing to start taking small steps that you can build upon each day. Starting to exercise, starting to eat better, watching less TV, and eliminating the things that keep nagging at you (for example, errands that need to be run and that unopened pile of mail on the counter that keeps staring at you).

Make a list of the little things you need to do, and start doing them. Completing and deleting them from your list will make you feel good. Going for a walk, cutting the lawn, doing some minor house repairs—they all count. And looking at what you managed to accomplish at the end of the day will boost your self-esteem and give you confidence that you're finally starting to make some progress at something.

This is how you get the ball rolling, but escaping from Retirement Hell requires more effort than that in the long run. You need to put some structure and routines back in your life. You need to find suitable replacements for the work friends you lost. You need to create a new identity for yourself and find new purpose.

Because in retirement you need to have a sense of purpose, a good reason to get out of bed in the morning. Without that, you will almost certainly start to decline. When you find a new way to contribute or help others—to matter again—you will live longer and feel better. When you have something to live for, it takes the stress away. It's not more complicated than that.

In the chapters that follow, we are going to show you what actions you need to take to escape Retirement Hell or even avoid it altogether, and get yourself to Retirement Heaven where you belong. I'm not going to lie to you—it won't be easy. The great things in life never are. But take it from me, the payoff is well worth the effort.

My Story

When I was forced out of my banking job after thirty-six years, I didn't follow the normal retirement progression and instead I went straight to Retirement Hell, which isn't a fun place, let me tell you. I was feeling the effects of Sudden Retirement Shock and kept having bad memories associated with work and how I was treated near the end.

The first thing I noticed was the strange silence that surrounded me during the week. My wife, "the Contessa," as I
affectionately call her, was still working and I was left alone at
home with nothing to do. With no more work email, there were
no self-assuring pings throughout the day. Nobody needed me
anymore, and my phone had also stopped ringing.

For the longest time I felt lost and had no energy to do anything. Things I used to enjoy, like fishing and riding my bike, no
longer interested me. Every night as I lay in bed, I worried if we
had saved up enough for retirement even though the Contessa,
who is an investment advisor, had told me we were OK financially. Thinking and worrying like that didn't make a lot of sense to
me. No, make that: *many* things at that point in my life no longer
made any sense to me.

Within a few short months of retiring,
Mike started to look like Howard Hughes...

I stopped looking after myself, didn't exercise, drank more than usual, and couldn't bother to shower every day. Why shower when you have no place to go? I just wanted to be left alone until I had a chance to heal. No one, not even the Contessa, who is very smart, could understand why I felt the way I did.

I felt alone and didn't feel like doing much of anything, until the day when my son Danny introduced me to some books written by Seth Godin. Those books really resonated with me and, over time, Seth became my virtual coach, challenging me to create the life I wanted to live. His daily inspirational blogs gave me the energy I needed and helped me overcome the fear that was holding me back, and hearing his keynote speech in person when he came to Toronto pushed me even more. He motivated me to create my own art (more on that concept in Chapter 15), and that is where the idea for writing *Victory Lap Retirement* came from.

Because of the retirement stress that I had been experiencing, I wasn't sleeping well and had gotten into a habit of getting up around 4:30 each morning, so I'd stagger over to my home office and start writing. The benefit of writing that early, well before your first cup of coffee, is that your conscious mind is still asleep and can't get in the way like it usually would. The unguarded truth comes out, which is soul-cleansing, and I always felt better after it. It was during those early writing episodes that I finally figured out what I wanted to do with the rest of my life.

But long before *Victory Lap Retirement* and even before discovering Seth Godin, I had a moment of epiphany thanks to one of my good old friends who gave me the opportunity to reconnect with myself and what was truly important to me.

Five Star Joe and Finding New Perspective

One day, while still suffering from retirement shock, I received a phone call from Five Star Joe, an old fishing buddy of mine who wanted me to go on a fishing trip for Atlantic salmon with him. Every year, Five Star goes with the same group of fishermen up to the George River, and one of the regulars couldn't make the trip that year. Normally I love fishing and would have jumped at the chance to go, but my retirement shock made me feel like doing nothing.

I was going to decline, but the Contessa thought going might help me get out of the funk I was in. She kept reminding me that Five Star Joe only went to the best places and so it was bound to be a really great experience. Soon I had visions of those famed fishing camps, like on the Miramachi River in Nova Scotia, where they have hot tubs, fine wines, and roast-beef carving stations. I finally weakened and agreed to go, but to be honest, my heart really wasn't into it and I didn't even bother to check out exactly where the lodge was.

It took us two days of traveling to get to the George River and I will never forget getting off the float plane. I was wearing shorts and it was very cold, even though the temperature was in the high eighties when we left Toronto. I asked one of the guides where the lodge was, and he said, "You're looking at it."

It was nothing like I had dreamed about. No hot tubs, no roast-beef carving stations, and at night I had trouble sleeping because of the cold Arctic air blowing through cracks between the logs. I started to whimper like a little kid, and that is when the first blackfly bit me. It was all downhill from there, and I cried myself to sleep that first night. I wanted to call the Contessa and have her find a way to get me out of there, but nothing works that far up north—no phones, no email, no texts—so I had no other option but to hang in for the duration.

At first it was hell: very cold and lonely, and I couldn't even watch TV. But by the third day, I started to feel a little better. Being up there with nothing else to do except sleep and fish gave me a chance to do some deep thinking. The isolation provided me with the opportunity to go deep inside myself. I realized I still had a long way to go in life, and I now had the freedom to do things that I could only dream about before when I was working. There were still a lot of things I wanted to accomplish before my time on this planet was done.

Visiting the George changed my perspective about things. I started to get my confidence back, and I knew my life was about to get a whole lot better. That trip, the one I was going to decline, changed me, and I've been going up there every year since. It's nice to have friends that care about you like Five Star Joe.

Create Your Own Retirement Heaven

When you know in advance what you can expect to go through in your retirement journey, you can plan ahead to avoid stages two and three altogether (Retirement Hell and the long, hard escape from it) and intentionally design and create a heavenly retirement for yourself, right from the start. Or, if you're already experiencing the Big Retirement Dip or you're stuck in Retirement Hell, you now have some perspective on why that is happening and what you can do about it. Wherever you're currently at in your life, the rest of the book is focused on helping you to design and create a life after work that is healthy, vibrant, and fulfilling.

Questions for Self-Reflection
- What are you going to do with your life when you finally have the freedom to do whatever you want to do?
- When do you want to retire, and why?
- What will you miss most about work?

- How will you substitute for the losses you feel?
- How will you create meaning in your life when you retire?
- If leaving work behind would be hard and stressful, why do it if you don't have to?

Simple Truths

- Significant change is an inevitable fact of retirement. How you choose to prepare for it and respond to it will determine if you will be happy or not.
- The stronger your connection to work, the harder will be your transition away from it, and the harder it will be to find contentment in retirement.
- If you are forced to retire, your transition into retirement is going to be longer and more difficult.
- Lack of structure and purpose hits some people hard.
- Full-stop retirement is unnatural for growth-oriented individuals. They are not wired to stop their lives at some arbitrary point after hitting a certain age.
- It's unhealthy to retire completely before your time.
- You can avoid Retirement Hell altogether by understanding what is coming your way and preparing for your retirement transition well in advance of leaving.
- You can escape Retirement Hell and get on the fast track toward Retirement Heaven by following the retirement principles that are outlined in Part Two.

2

Recharge and Recalibrate

All endings are also beginnings. We just don't know it at the time.
—*Mitch Albom*

Because of all the stress endured over their working years, many people are physically and mentally worn out when they retire. If you happen to fall into this category, you will need to take a break once you stop working so that you can reduce your stress level, recover, and get your head back on straight before getting into any of the serious stuff of self-examination and planning your future, which starts later in this chapter and continues throughout the book.

Until you feel strong and your confidence returns, you are less likely to do the things you need to do to be successful in retirement. Chances are, you will not work out, you will not eat healthy, and you certainly will not feel equipped to discover your mission or plan for the future until you've given yourself some much-needed TLC. You will keep coming up with excuses why you can't start—until you feel recovered and decide that it's finally time to start the climb out of Retirement Hell.

It's hard to think clearly about what you want to do with the rest of your life if you are worn out, depressed, or stressed out. If this is how you're feeling, you should avoid putting too many expectations on yourself or setting too many goals at first. Until you are ready, it's hard to generate the "wantpower" required to do the things necessary to achieve retirement success. For now, be patient and kind to yourself until you find the strength and motivation to transform your life from being aimlessly hellish to being a vibrant and fulfilling Victory Lap.

When you are taking good care of both your body and your mind, you have more energy, you are more resilient, and you are mentally stronger to face the challenges that lie ahead. So, focus on getting physically and mentally fit. And start doing some of the things that you've always liked and wanted to do, but don't be surprised if they aren't enjoyable for a while.

Getting Started: Introducing Some New Routines

There are some proven coping strategies that can help you adapt to all the sudden changes that you will be experiencing. It's hard to stay mentally upbeat when everything you have known as normal is upended. These methods helped me recover from the shock I was suffering from when I retired completely and abruptly, and they gave me the inner strength I needed to get back on my feet.

Practice Active Meditation

Some people have no trouble practicing meditation in the traditional way, but for me, sitting quietly and still in a room alone, assuming certain body positions, utilizing special items like incense and candles just doesn't feel real. What I found works for me are various types of active meditation, such as fishing, running, taking a shower, riding my bike, lane swimming, and watering my lawn in the early morning. Anywhere I can tune out the day-to-day noise and reflect on things while I'm engaged in a physical activity gives me focus, calm, and clarity of mind. It is during these times that I come up with some of my most creative ideas and solutions.

The benefits of meditation, however you choose to do it, are many:

- It helps you to focus and stay in the moment.
- It opens up your mind to receive new information and ideas.
- It relaxes you and relieves stress.
- It helps you develop and maintain a positive attitude about yourself and your circumstances.

LESSONS FROM A PANDEMIC

The COVID-19 pandemic put our nervous systems into overdrive. Watching the daily updates on the exponential growth in infections and the rising number of deaths caused acute stress and anxiety in many of us. Some people turned to alcohol and cannabis for relief, but the smart ones turned to various forms of mindfulness, such as meditation and yoga, which allowed them to take a pause and reset themselves in the midst of the chaos. If it can work in such an extreme global crisis, it can help you get into a calm, positive frame of mind to deal with the challenges of retirement planning.

Keep a Daily Journal and a Daily Log

There are two key notebooks that I keep in the top drawer of my desk and that I use and refer to on a regular basis. My journal is for personal exploration, and it's where I do my deep thinking. My daily log is for planning purposes. It contains my goals and schedule for the week and for the year, and I also use it to track my daily activity and progress. Let's review the important role of the daily journal first.

Journaling: A Book by You, About You

When was the last time you really went deep and connected with yourself? If you're like most, it's probably been a long time. It's hard to connect with yourself when you are stressed out and busy with day-to-day living. Journaling in a quiet spot either in the late evening or early morning removes the noise and distractions that consume you, and allows you to go deep inside yourself so you can reconnect with your authentic self and hear your inner voice.

> Stay true to yourself and listen to your inner voice. It will lead you to your dream.
>
> —James Ross

Your journal is your private place where your mind can play and have some fun daydreaming about what is possible for you in retirement. While journaling, you will begin to discover new interests, desires, and direction. You might reawaken long-lost dreams and passions, or you might discover something new that you are really excited about trying.

Journaling also helps with the healing process and allows you to open up, exposing to yourself things you may have been hiding or avoiding. Maybe you are embarrassed about how you look or feel, or maybe you're embarrassed to tell people how scared you are about losing your work identity and starting life over with a blank slate in retirement, or maybe you're nervous about applying for that part-time job you want.

When journaling, don't use your computer; it's best to write by hand. Putting your thoughts in words on paper, or even doodling them out, will trigger a number of thoughts and feelings. You will begin thinking and dreaming at a deeper level, and that is when the magic starts.

Your journal is the place where you first test your ideas out, and the more you write, the more you will get a sense of what you need to do. It is during these "quiet times" that you can turn off your conscious mind, which likes to scare us by reminding us of our limitations, making us think and worry way too much.

Your inner voice knows you better than your brain does because thoughts and answers to tough questions are coming from the real you, without being filtered and censored by your rational brain. Through the introspective process of journaling on a regular basis, you will discover that most of the answers you are looking for are already inside you. While writing, ask yourself what you need to do in order to be happy in retirement; you will probably be surprised by some of the stuff that comes back at you. In my case, more than once I would start writing about something and, suddenly, I would veer way off course and go deep into something I wasn't even consciously thinking about.

Your inner voice knows what your true mission is and wants you to start taking action. Until you do, it will keep sending you messages and clues. Listen to your inner voice—your intuition, your gut. What is it telling you? Be patient and listen, and it will point you in the direction you need to go. To encourage your inner voice to come to the fore, ask yourself the questions that appear in each chapter. Keep asking yourself those same questions, and over time the answers will come to you.

> Your life is always speaking to you. The fundamental spiritual question is: Will you listen?
>
> — Oprah Winfrey

In Part 3 we'll look at some specific techniques to help you discover your mission and values so that you can begin the work of planning what you want for yourself in retirement; for now, just get into the habit of journaling to tap in to your inner voice. This will make it easier for you to discover your true mission and for concrete plans for your future to begin bubbling to the surface, which is when the heavy lifting begins.

Warning: It's a big mistake not to listen to and follow what your inner voice is trying to tell you. If you choose to ignore it, you will be left with an emptiness inside, a sense of regret that you will have to live with for the rest of your life.

Benefits of listening to your inner voice while journaling:

- It will help you recover from Sudden Retirement Shock.
- It will help you let go of soul-sucking grudges.
- It will help you understand what you are meant to do and will give you a good sense of what you are capable of.
- It will remind you about what you like, what you don't like, and what you need to do in order to be happy.
- It will give you a heads up when you go against your values and beliefs. You will start to feel uncomfortable and your inner voice, acting as your personal GPS, will tell you that you are off course and need to make a course correction.
- It will help you set challenging and inspiring goals for your retirement and push you to take action.
- It will give you confidence to do what you plan on doing.

You will find your inner voice getting louder when:

- you start dreaming about what is possible,
- you start believing in yourself and what you have planned for retirement, and
- you start doing what you are passionate about and feel you were born to do.

Questions for Self-Reflection:
- Can you hear your inner voice?
- Ask it questions you need answers to. What is it telling you?
- What is holding you back from living a happy, healthy, fulfilling retirement?
- What does your dream retirement look like?
- What are you looking forward to?
- When will you start keeping a daily journal? How about right now?

Daily Log: Set Goals and Measure Your Progress

While your journal is a place for you to record your dreams, fears, and innermost feelings, your daily log is a practical tool that will help you take steps to achieve your dreams, overcome your deep-seated worries, and work your way toward a happy, healthy, fulfilling Retirement Heaven.

Use your log to monitor whatever you feel it is important to take action on, the things you want to change to improve your life: your weight, workouts, diet, level of happiness, time usage, activities, attitude—whatever you feel the need to work on. At the end of every day, use your log to record your daily activity, to create awareness of how you are spending your time, and to recognize to what extent you are addressing your new priorities.

Using your log will:

- indicate whether your day was a productive one or not,
- indicate if you are staying on track with your goals,
- give you ideas about how you can improve things going forward, and
- serve as your conscience. Did you give today your best shot and are you doing the things you need to do to stay/ get healthy and boost your happiness?

By going back over your log, you will be able to see how much you have already accomplished, which is a big help when you are going through a rough patch and start doubting yourself. Keeping a log may seem like a fairly superficial exercise at first glance, but trust me, once you start using it regularly you will find that it's an important tool in keeping you on track with your objectives and boosting your confidence to take proactive steps to pull yourself out of Retirement Hell.

Long Solo Walks Daily

Long walks are therapeutic on a number of levels. Not only are they good exercise, they also serve as a great opportunity for informal meditation and practicing mindfulness. They give you the physical and mental space to think, to contemplate, and to enjoy just being out in nature, breathing the fresh air and being in the moment.

Often, you'll find that on these walks, you will focus on some of the things you wrote about in your journal earlier that morning or the day before, and the quiet time alone will help you come up with possible solutions to the challenges you are facing. It's just you alone with your thoughts, a special time when you get to ask yourself questions and receive answers.

To get the most out of your walks, allocate a minimum of thirty minutes. And get rid of your phone or other electronics so you have no distractions or interruptions. (If you prefer to take your phone in case of emergency, then simply put it on silent.)

Regular brisk walking will deliver some significant benefits to you:

- It can lower your risk for high blood pressure, high cholesterol, diabetes, and certain types of cancers.
- It will improve/maintain your mobility.

- It increases your energy level and makes you feel good.
- It helps you clear your mind, lower your stress, think better, and lose weight all at the same time.

Before you start a vigorous walking program or a more intense exercise routine, be sure to visit your doctor and have him or her do a complete checkup. One of the main objectives of any training program is to get fit and get your health back, so be prepared to sweat a little.

In fact, when you embark on the process of self-examination followed by planning for and achieving a rewarding retirement, be prepared to sweat both literally and figuratively. Physical exercise is an important component of keeping (or getting) fit and increasing your energy levels, and the soul-searching you'll be doing to design and attain your own little piece of Retirement Heaven will make you sweat mentally. Designing and running your Victory Lap is not easy work, but believe me, it is so worth it! Again, we'll get into the details of how to do all this later in parts 3 and 4.

Purge the Bad Stuff: Let go of Grudges and Guilt

I love that quote from Nelson Mandela because it is so true.

Holding a grudge is an ego thing and one of the most stressful, unproductive, and time-wasting activities you can do. Even worse, it can wreak havoc on your body, leading to high blood pressure and heart disease. Why continue to punish yourself by reliving perceived injustices over and over again in your mind? It doesn't make a lot of sense, does it?

> Holding a grudge is like drinking poison and hoping the other guy will die.
>
> —Nelson Mandela

An important step on the road to Retirement Heaven is to purge your mind and spirit of all the bad stuff that has built up in your head over the years. It would be easy to do this if someone were to develop a brain detoxifier that would eliminate all that negativity, but until that happens, we will have to rely on journaling, additional forms of active meditation, and other good habits to help purge our minds of our toxic thoughts and feelings.

During journaling, in addition to your hopes and dreams for retirement, you will also write about and work through your bad work memories, your regrets, and your fears. You need to dig down and bring up all the bad stuff to the surface so that it can be reviewed and finally let go. Until you deal with all the bad stuff that happened to you and learn to get over it, your brain will keep going over and over it until it drives you a little crazy. It's best to confront it now so you can move on to the good stuff.

If you were pushed out of a job like I was, for example, you need to accept what happened and understand that it was not your fault. Corporate decisions are driven by business strategy, cost reductions, and other factors beyond your control—not because they want to stick it to you. They did not necessarily let you go because they thought you were not good enough, so don't look at what happened as a reflection on you and your abilities. It was just business, so try to accept it for what it is and don't take it personally anymore. You can't begin to move on with a healthy frame of mind without first letting go of any negative thoughts you have.

To help you do that, try writing a goodbye letter to your old company or boss and say all the things you need or want to finally say to gain closure. After writing it, put it away for a few days and then read it again. Reading that letter will make you smile, realizing what a fool you have been, letting such things get to you for so long.

*Mike wondered if he would ever have any **good** dreams about work.*

My Story

I didn't like the way things ended for me at the bank. I was forced out, which as many of you know, is never fun. Although, I was happy about it in one regard, because I wanted a way out anyway, and so what they did just accelerated my departure date with the added bonus of a severance check in my pocket.

It's not what they did, but how they did it that really bothered me. One day while visiting my boss in his office, he asked me to go with him up to the boardroom to go over that year's profit plan. Upon entering the room, I noticed a lady around my son's age sitting alone at the table with a file in front of her, and then the process started. This cloak-and-dagger approach with the surprise ending left a bad taste in my mouth because I felt there was no respect involved, and it just felt so wrong after faithfully working for the company all those years. Respect and honesty are big values of mine so, yes, the way they did it bothered me for a while.

Even though they forced me out, part of the deal was that I wasn't supposed to tell anyone. The bank wanted me to pretend that I was retiring, and they gave me a party along with the traditional retirement card. Now, don't get me wrong, I love a good party, but the thought of going there felt kind of weird to me, like attending my own funeral, and I toyed with the idea of not showing up. To add insult to injury, there were some other people retiring at the same time, so the company decided to lump all the parties together to make things easier. Talk about feeling special.

In the end, I forced myself to go. I remember thinking, I just need to get through this retirement party and I'm out of here. I ended up leaving before everyone else, shaking the hands of the people I liked and avoiding everyone else. It's hard to have a good time even at your own retirement party when it's not authentic.

I've thought a lot on this, and traditional retirement parties have it all wrong. When you think about other celebrations in our lives like weddings and birthdays, they are all about the future. The focus is not on what you have done but, rather, on what you plan to do. Our current template for a retirement party sounds more like a wake or funeral, the only difference being that the guest of honor is not in a coffin.

I wish I could have left my company on a happier note, but please don't feel sorry for me, because as you will learn, my life was about to get a whole lot better.

On that note, remember that retirement shock is a state of mind, and one of the easiest ways to rid yourself of it is simply to decide not to retire in the traditional sense. Your stress will fall away if you view leaving your primary career as the opportunity that it really is: after so many years, you are finally free again to find new purpose and recreate yourself. Your goal should be to

Mike was robbed in the parking lot after leaving his retirement party, but instead of money, all they got was his identity.

find something that can replace what you lost by leaving work behind—something better, something that gets you excited to get out of bed in the morning. Believe me, it's out there, you just have to go find it.

Feelings of guilt work just like grudges; they are two sides of the same coin and have the same effect on your psyche and your physical well-being, eating you up and holding you back if you don't deal with them. And guilt can take many forms. For example, guilt that you could have been a better father and helped around the house more if you hadn't always let work get in the way; guilt that you lost contact with some of your friends because you were busy with other things; guilt that you are not doing more with your life and enjoying the retirement you dreamed of. Like grudges, you need to let these feelings go before they end up messing up your life. It's not too late to do this; you still have time to fix things.

LESSONS FROM A PANDEMIC

As we know, there are some positive things that came out of the COVID-19 pandemic and, for me, one of them was that it made me finally make the call.

For a number of reasons, my relationship with my brother had soured over the years, and when our mother passed away I didn't think we would ever talk again—our relationship was that bad. It's not that my brother didn't try to fix things; he did try, but I couldn't let things from the past go. I couldn't forgive him because I didn't feel he deserved forgiveness. This festering grudge and our unresolved feelings caused me a great deal of stress and anxiety for years.

Then, one day during the pandemic I began wondering how he was doing and if he was safe from the coronavirus. I thought it was crazy not being able to talk to one another, and it got me thinking about the regret I would feel if something ever happened to him.

I decided to make the call and forgive my brother, not because I felt he deserved it, but because I deserved it. I forgave him because I wanted to be free of the sadness and anger and resentment. I knew in my heart it was the right thing to do and, while it wasn't easy, just knowing that I made the effort to fix things freed me from feeling a lot of regret and guilt.

Are you harboring anger, resentment, or other hard feelings toward someone? Have you avoided talking to them for a long time? Then you know what you need to do: you need to fix things before it is too late, so you can avoid a ton of regret that will be coming your way if you don't. Make the call like I did and forgive them, because you deserve it. Trust me, you will feel much better after you do.

Going through the purge isn't easy. It's equivalent to what you went through if you ever tried to quit smoking. Your body and your mind will experience high levels of stress, and you will find it difficult to stay the course. You will begin to doubt yourself and wonder if it's really worth it. Keep journaling and writing in your log every day to work through the tough stuff. It really will help.

Questions for Self-Reflection
- Did you achieve proper closure with your old job?
- Are you still reliving the past instead of looking ahead and planning for the future?
- Are there things you feel guilty or angry about?
- Do you hold any grudges?
- What bad experiences or feelings do you need to let go of?
- Are you relieved to have retired but anxious about what that really means?
- Do you miss the structure of your work life, your work friends, and the sense of purpose and accomplishment you got from working? Do you worry about how you'll replace all that?
- What do you want to do now that you are free again?
- What tools will you use to help purge any negativity you harbor so that you can move forward? Will you commit to a daily journal, a daily log, meditation, mindfulness, and/or solitary walks?

Simple Truths
- Many times, a job loss can be a great gain.
- Listen to your gut. It's smarter than you are.
- Change is scary, even the good kind.
- You can't drift your way to a great retirement.
- Have hope knowing that there is still time to have the life you always dreamed about. It is still out there waiting for you. You just need to reach out and grab it!
- Forgiveness is a simple choice to make but not always easy to do, especially when we feel we are right.
- It's important to give yourself a break and recover before planning your transition into Victory Lap. You think and plan better when you are not physically/mentally worn out.

PART 2

THE NINE RETIREMENT PRINCIPLES

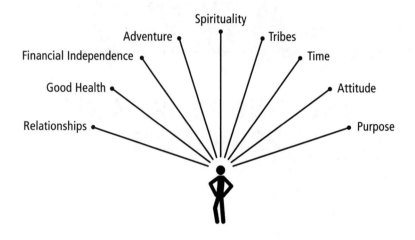

3

Nine Principles for an Exceptional Retirement

Principles are fundamental truths that serve as the foundations for behavior that gets you what you want out of life. They can be applied again and again in similar situations to help you achieve your goals.
—Ray Dalio

A successful retirement doesn't just happen because you have a lot of money and a lot of stuff. Lifestyle and attitude have a lot more to do with how happy you are in this stage of your life, and so does aligning that lifestyle with your personal values, as we will see in detail in Part 3. No matter how much money you have to fund your lifestyle and how much financial planning you do to prepare for retirement, there are many challenges and obstacles that can stand in the way of feeling fulfilled at this stage of your life. These include not having a good attitude, not challenging your brain, not being physically active, not having strong relationships with family and friends, not having a sense of purpose, and not eating healthy. If not addressed, these problems are going to cost you big-time.

The good news is that we have far more influence over our retirement future than we realize. Research has shown that longevity is impacted up to 80 percent by a person's chosen lifestyle. For years I've studied successful retirees and what they have in common in terms of their attitude and lifestyle choices. Based on what I've learned from them, in addition to my other research and my personal observations and retirement experiences, I've identified nine key principles that are essential to achieving a heavenly retirement. The principles are as follows:

1. Nurture Strong Relationships
2. Foster Good Health
3. Achieve Financial Independence
4. Reignite Your Sense of Adventure
5. Tap into Your Spirituality
6. Find Your Tribes
7. Make the Most of Your Time
8. Adopt the Right Attitude
9. Discover Your Purpose

We'll look at each of these principles in detail in the nine chapters that follow; for now, just know that they are foundational for retirement success, and by following them you have the opportunity to slow age-related decline and enjoy a vibrant, happy retirement.

The beauty of all nine retirement principles is that they can be effective for everyone, no matter how much you have managed to save for retirement. They are fundamental truths that, if followed, will empower you to make good decisions for your future and optimize the quality of your retirement so you can live your best and happiest life. They will

> We control our actions, but the consequences that flow from those actions are controlled by principles.
>
> —Stephen Covey

influence your lifestyle, your habits, your goals, and your choices. Only with these guiding principles in place can you focus on getting the big things in retirement right.

As you go through the nine principles chapter by chapter, you will notice that they are interlinked and support each other, which means that when you do well in one area, it will positively impact how well you do in in relation to one or more of the other principles.

Rating Your Performance on the Principles

At the end of each chapter covering the nine principles, we will ask you to rank your satisfaction with that principle on a scale of 1–10, where 10 represents the highest score, to see how well you are currently following it. You will then be asked to write down two to three strategies that you intend to use to improve the rating of that principle in your life.

From Principles to Action

Once you have a good understanding of the principles and how they play off each other, you then need to come up with your own plan for how best to integrate them into your life. For instance, Retirement Principle #9 is about finding a purpose, and you might choose to accomplish this by starting up your own small business or perhaps through volunteering in support of a good cause.

Purpose is, in fact, such an important guiding principle that all of Part 3 is dedicated to the how-to of tapping into your passions and values to define your personal mission. Then, in Part 4 we focus on retirement lifestyle design—the practical aspects of planning how exactly you will fulfill that mission in your Victory Lap.

The process is the same for everyone, but the specific goals you choose and the path you decide to take to achieve them will be particular to you. With the nine retirement principles at the foundation of the process, retirement lifestyle design turns your goals into action and a plan that's right for you—a plan that gets you to the heavenly retirement you desire.

So, with all this in mind, let's get started.

4

Retirement Principle #1

Nurture Strong Relationships

When you are in the final days of your life, what will you want?
Will you hug that college degree in the walnut frame? Will you ask
to be carried to the garage so you can sit in your car? Will you find
comfort in rereading your financial statement? Of course not. What
will matter then will be people. If relationships will matter most then,
shouldn't they matter most now?
   — Max Lucado

In his best-selling book *Outliers*, Malcolm Gladwell talks about the magical town of Roseto in eastern Pennsylvania. The town was established when a group of people from Roseto, Italy, immigrated to the United States looking for a better life in the late 1890s. When they sent word back home about the exciting possibilities that existed in the States, more and more people immigrated to the new town they of course named New Roseto, which ended up looking and feeling just like the town they left back home.

New Roseto was its own tiny, self-sufficient world. The people spoke Italian and kept mostly to themselves, farming or working in the local slate quarry. One day, a curious doctor noticed that in Roseto it was rare for people under the age of sixty-five to suffer from heart disease. This was in stark contrast to the rest of the US population at the time. What made Roseto even more interesting is that it was a place where people didn't follow the recommended healthy-living guidelines we live by today, yet they died from heart attacks at roughly half the rate of the rest of America. Something didn't make sense. Or did it?

At first, researchers thought that the people of New Roseto must have brought over from Italy a lifestyle that was superior to that practiced by the average American, but they were wrong. The Rosetans smoked heavily, drank wine with abandon, and didn't follow the healthy Mediterranean diet of olive oil, light salads, and mostly fish and chicken for protein. Instead they ate high-fat salami and various cheeses all brimming with cholesterol, and they fried their sausages and meatballs in artery-clogging lard. The Rosetans also did not like to exercise much. In fact, many were struggling with obesity.

The next theory proposed to explain the town's miraculous health—genetics—was also wrong. Rosetans who left town and lived in other parts of the United States experienced higher rates of heart disease than the people who remained in town.

After exhausting all the possibilities, the researchers concluded that the reason the Rosetans could do everything wrong—eat all the wrong foods, be overweight, smoke—and still live longer than most was because of Roseto itself.

The Rosetans had transferred the culture of Southern Italy to their new home in Pennsylvania, and that culture was able to shield them from the pressures of everyday America. Their health was nourished by the strong family and community relationships around them, and because of this they were happy and less stressed than people elsewhere.

The Rosetans spent time sitting on their porches speaking to whoever happened to pass by. For the Rosetans, family was everything, and many of the homes in town had three generations of the same family living in them. Unlike common practice in many other US communities, the elderly were neither institutionalized nor marginalized; they grew old with dignity and love, surrounded by family.

Outside the home, the people of the town participated in an incredible number of civic organizations that they created. Even though there were bigger stores in nearby towns, the people were loyal to their own small local shops. If they needed a new suit, they automatically went to see "Tony the Tailor," the same place their father and grandfather shopped.

In Roseto, it was hard to tell who was rich or poor. People who had money didn't display their wealth; they lived like everyone else, which meant there was no urge to compete and keep up with the Joneses. On Sundays, everyone went to mass at the same church. They had strong Christian values and were very spiritual people.

This real-life story shows us the benefits of living life with low levels of stress and anxiety. Rosetans didn't spend much time worrying about things, because their lives were stable and predictable. They knew that there would always be a roof over their heads and food on the table, and they didn't worry about losing their job because they knew they could always find work at the local slate quarry. They put their worries into God's hands and could sleep well at night knowing that whatever happened, their family and community would always be there to help in bad times. Because of that, there was no suicide, no alcoholism, and no drug addiction, and there was a zero-crime rate.

Roseto Today

This is the part that Malcolm Gladwell didn't tell us about in his book. Maybe he just didn't want to depress us. Because, sadly, today's Rosetans experience the same rates of heart disease as everyone else. Over the years, they became more Americanized, which translates into being much less close as a community and much more stressed.

When the first-generation Rosetans died, their children strayed away from the "old ways"; the strong social ties and protection that family and community offered. The kids felt the need to own their own homes. Families split up and suburbanization occurred, with the development of single-family homes with fenced-in yards.

The pursuit of wealth and materialism became commonplace. Wealthy Rosetans came out of hiding and began to flaunt their wealth and started driving fancier cars. People no longer went to the Marconi Social Club; they went to the new country club instead. This caused stress for the less well-off, who tried to keep up with their neighbors but couldn't. All this stress started to add up, and in 1971, the first person under age forty-five died of a heart attack in Roseto.

What Can We Learn from the Story of Roseto?

The story of the Rosetans reminds us of the toll that modern life exacts from us. It teaches us that longevity is not just about healthy food choices or how much we exercise or having favorable genes. The truth is that the people we surround ourselves with and make time for have a profound effect on both our health and our happiness. You could have all the money you ever wanted, but without loving relations, you won't be happy, and it's hard to be healthy when you're unhappy.

There is something magical about having people to talk to, people who care about you. Knowing that they will be there for you in a time of need helps increase your resiliency. This is why we made the importance of having strong relationships the first of our nine retirement principles.

It's a sad fact that today many of us have been so busy dealing with life and work that we don't really know the people living around us. Over time, we have lost touch with our neighbors and our community—often even our family—and that chosen isolation will cost us large in retirement. No man is an island. No one thrives in isolation.

To enjoy a happy and fulfilling retirement, we need to re-think our lives and invest more time with our family, friends, and community, like the original Rosetans did. We are all hardwired with the need for belonging, but today we are slowly losing our sense of connectedness because traditional sources of social connectedness in the form of community organizations, religious groups, and so on are in steady decline. Because of new technology, most of us are no longer connected in the way we need to be, and that can negatively impact the quality of our retirement.

Every day, we are feeling more alone as more and more leisure activities are becoming solitary: watching TV, being immersed in social media, working on the computer, and playing computer games on our smartphones. We might have thousands of friends on Facebook that like our posts, but this is a poor substitute for good old-fashioned in-person interaction.

Over the course of my research, I have learned:

- Social isolation increases the risk of premature death by an eye-opening 30 percent, and some estimates have it as high as 60 percent, which means that loneliness might be a more significant health factor than obesity, smoking, exercise, or nutrition.

- Loneliness and isolation, as described by Julianne Holt-Lunstad, a professor of psychology at Brigham Young University, are equivalent to the health risk of smoking fifteen cigarettes a day, which is bad—especially if you're a non-smoker.
- Loneliness raises blood pressure and levels of the stress hormone cortisol, increasing your chances of a heart attack or stroke.
- Loneliness weakens a person's immune system, which decreases the ability to fight cancers and other illnesses, making you vulnerable to all types of medical problems including heart disease.
- Loneliness increases your risk for dementia and Alzheimer's.
- Sadly, today 50 percent of older people say that TV is their main source of company.
- Over 51 percent of people age seventy-five and over live alone.

Loneliness Can Kill You

I've seen this firsthand. My uncle, after he divorced late in life, isolated himself and had only one friend who he associated with, my father. When my father died, I knew my uncle would have a hard time adjusting, and sure enough, he passed away a couple of years later. Sad but true: loneliness can kill you over time.

If you only had time for work friends when you were working, don't be surprised if you find yourself suddenly alone soon after retiring. We mistakenly view friendships at work as real friends, but the majority of them are not. Many of these relationships don't last when the corporate glue that binds is gone. This could be even worse if you were managing people, because when you retire, those people won't be a part of your daily life like they were, and you will feel like your value to others is no longer there.

For those reasons, one of the biggest mistakes you can make is not working hard enough on creating true friendships outside of the workplace. If you feel that you truly have a connection with some of your work friends, the ones who take an interest in you, take the time to invest in and deepen these relationships before you retire.

LESSONS FROM A PANDEMIC

The COVID-19 pandemic highlighted the importance of the loving relationships we have with family, friends, and community. It was comforting to know that there were people who cared about us and were there in this time of need.

Perhaps more than anything, the crisis reinforced how much we all crave social connection and physical contact with those we love. Phone calls and video calls got us through, but what people missed most was interacting with other people. We all missed the real in-person thing, and the first thing people did after leaving self-isolation was to hug their family.

One important thing the pandemic reminded me of is that, under normal circumstances, we do not spend enough quality time having meaningful conversations with our family, especially with our kids. Before the pandemic hit, everyone was so busy doing their own thing. Most conversations with our kids were superficial because everyone was in a hurry to get on to the next thing. The pandemic gave us the time to go deeper in our conversations, understand things better, and reconnect. Hopefully this lesson will last way after the crisis is over.

True Friends

Life is hard, and so you want to make sure you don't have to go through it alone. True friends are special and will always be there in times of need, no matter how long it has been since you've last seen them or how many miles away they might be. They are the ones you know have your back—the ones you can call at two in

> A friend is one who knows all about you and likes you anyway.
> —Christi Mary Warner

the morning for help. It's a big mistake to neglect true friendships, so be sure to make an effort to keep in contact with your closest friends as much as possible. They will become even more important as you grow older.

Fact: Most men are not very good at making friends and often have fewer close friends than women; this will cost them in terms of their degree of loneliness when they retire. In a 2016 survey conducted by UK's Movember organization, over half of the men surveyed reported having two or less friends they could discuss "something deeply personal with," and 19 percent of men over fifty-five said they lacked a close friend at all.

Ways to make new friends:

- Join a tribe that has similar interests to you, or better yet, start your own. (See Chapter 9, Retirement Principle #6: Find Your Tribes, for more on this idea.)
- Volunteering will connect you to others with similar values.
- Playing sports or engaging in hobbies you enjoy are great ways to connect with others.
- Creating a blog allows you to connect with others who have passions or interests similar to yours.

It's also important to understand the difference between real friends and your children. Everyone talks about the importance of maintaining a close relationship with their kids, but the truth is that it's your friends who will most likely provide you with the most enjoyment in your Victory Lap.

When your children leave one day to begin their own families, you will spend most of your time hanging out with your friends. These are the people who understand what you are going through because they are experiencing the same things themselves. They can offer moral and emotional support with health issues, boredom, mobility issues, and loneliness after losing a spouse.

Friends also have a positive effect on your behaviors. People tend to take better care of themselves when they hang around with people who care about them. Friends will remind you to take your pills, encourage you to get out more, and guilt you into adopting healthier habits or at least moderating bad ones. Lonely people who do not have someone holding them accountable tend to eat worse, get less exercise, and spend most of their day sitting on the couch binge-watching Netflix.

Having a good support network of real friends is extremely valuable to staying healthy. So, choose your friends well. Pick the fun ones; the ones who are passionate and a little crazy. Also spend some time hanging around young people—they will help you to keep thinking young as well as possibly be with you at a point in your life when some of your older friends may not.

Mattering Matters

When you work, you matter. You have a purpose, a focus; and you are relied upon by your employer. Knowing you matter makes you feel good because it

> A life is not important except in the impact it has on other lives.
>
> —Jackie Robinson

satisfies an innate need. But the day after you retire, your smartphone will go silent. The emails and texts will stop rolling in, and it will feel like you are not part of anything anymore.

When you retire, you need to find something new to replace the strong sense of connection, of mattering in some way, or you are always going to feel empty inside. Following are some suggested ways to feel that you matter.

- Continue working in some way: This could be by running your own business or consultancy, working part-time, or doing volunteer work.
- Contribute to the community: Again, volunteering is a great way to do this; or join a theater group, residents association, or mentoring group.
- Nurture relationships with family and friends: Your closest relationships will sustain and support you more than most others.
- Find your tribe(s): Spending time with like-minded people who share your passions, whether they involve sports, hobbies, education, culture, travel—there are endless ways to feel connected over common interests.

Questions for Self-Reflection
- Who depends on you to be in their lives?
- Who can you depend on in a time of need?
- What do you do that is appreciated and valued by others?
- How much would you be missed if you went away?

Gray Divorce: How Retirement Can Screw Up a Good Marriage

If you have a partner, that person is likely the closest relationship you have in your life; the person to whom you matter most and the one with whom you have been sharing your retirement dreams, perhaps for decades. If this describes your situation, you need to take special note that divorce rates for seniors are on the rise, and the highest percentage for divorce is currently in the fifty-five-to-sixty-four age category. Divorcing at this age can destroy the two of you both emotionally and financially, so you better take whatever actions necessary to ensure this doesn't happen to you.

Studies have shown that transitioning to retirement usually produces a temporary decline in marital satisfaction for both partners, which isn't surprising when you think about it. It's sad to see this happen to couples after all the sacrifices that both of them made. Instead of enjoying the payoff from all the years of hard work, they find themselves talking about possible divorce instead. If you find yourself having discussions like this with your partner upon retirement, you can hope it's temporary instead of a rift that will tear your relationship apart, or you can work to overcome it or, better yet, avoid it in the first place.

When you were both working, the needs of your kids and your jobs came before everything else. Because each of you was so busy working and ferrying your kids to various activities and appointments, you both ended up spending a good portion of the day leading independent lives. This changes when you retire: the alone time disappears, and many retirees have trouble adjusting to the increased togetherness.

Together Again, for Better or Worse

When you retire and things slow down, you have more time to think about things, and this is when old existing problems with relationships start to bubble to the surface. People start to see things they didn't notice before. The "why" that held the two of you together for so many years—the kid(s)—is gone, and so is the financial pressure to provide for your family. As you spend more time with only your significant other, you might begin to realize that you really don't have a lot of things in common anymore; the two of you grew apart over the years when your focus was on work and kids instead of on each other and your relationship.

LESSONS FROM A PANDEMIC

According to news reports in Xi'an, a city of twelve million people in China that was placed in lockdown during the COVID-19 crisis, divorce applications spiked when restraints were lifted. I wasn't surprised by this and I expect to see the same thing occur in both the United States and Canada when the results come in. Whether it be due to retirement or a pandemic, many couples have trouble adjusting to the increased togetherness, which can put a strain on any relationship.

You need to create a new environment in which you're able to reconnect and you both can flourish, and you need to do this fast, because when it comes to retirement, how well you and your partner get along will have the biggest impact on your health and happiness.

Some common retirement relationship mistakes:

1. **Having poor communication.** Thinking only about yourself and what you want to do in retirement is one of the biggest mistakes you can make. Many newly retired couples are unaware of their partner's preferences and end up being blindsided by differences in retirement dreams, plans, and expectations. What do you want to do? What does your partner want to do? Where do you want to live? Where does your partner want to live? What's on your bucket list? What's on theirs? If there are major differences, you both need to find a way of getting on the same page fast, to ensure a smooth retirement transition. Talk about some of your ideas and concerns, and when your partner talks about theirs, don't be

negative or quick to shoot them down. Be open and share your thoughts and concerns with each other and be clear about what is important to each of you and why.

2. **Not understanding what your partner is going through**. Even if your partner didn't work outside the home, they will struggle with your retirement just as much as you do, and they don't even get to feel retired, because the day-to-day housework and family responsibilities never end. For the longest time, their needs were secondary to the demands of your career, and while you were working at the Corp, they created an identity and independent life of their own. The home is their domain and they are accustomed to a lot of privacy, autonomy, and time with their friends. It's a mistake to expect your partner to change all their routines for you when you do retire. If you constantly criticize them and try to control them, things aren't going to work out so well.

3. **Guilting your partner into retiring because you feel lonely or sorry for yourself**. Men typically retire before their partner, and those who do often battle more loneliness if their spouse is still working. But you will regret forcing your partner to leave something that they really enjoy before they are ready. They could hold that against you forever—and forever is a long time!

   Just because you're retiring doesn't automatically mean that your partner wants or needs to retire along with you. It really depends on what you each want. Some couples plan on retiring at the same time because they like doing most things together. Some people prefer to retire separately; that is, one person still wants to continue working while the other is retired, and there is nothing wrong with that if they are getting a lot of meaning and satisfaction from their work. There are so many ways of doing it successfully, again, provided that you are on the same page and have bought into the same plan, whatever it is.

4. **Allowing yourself to become a victim of your partner's retirement lifestyle**. You don't want to go from being an active achiever, someone who is happy to be always on the go but who, in retirement, morphs into your spouse, becoming a couch potato filling your days with watching TV. Conversely, if your partner leads a super active life, don't feel like you have to get involved in every activity they take part in on a daily basis if that's not what makes you happy. You don't have to do everything together in retirement, and nor should you. You need to give each other some space to grow. Everyone needs their private time, and both of you need to understand that.

5. **Leaning heavily on your partner for support because all your work friends are gone**. Men usually have a harder time adjusting to retirement because they don't know what to do with themselves or with all the spare time they have on their hands when they lose their work. Because they were so busy climbing up the corporate ladder and taking care of their family, they had little time to develop outside interests or leisure activities. And so, when they retire and lose their customer relationships along with their work friends and colleagues, their relationship with their partner is the only thing they can lean on. As discussed previously, men have a harder time making friends and developing

new social networks. An increase in loneliness can cause them to follow their partner around like lost puppies in retirement, as they lean on their partner to serve as both their best friend and entertainment event coordinator. Newly retired men risk intruding on their spouse's territory and routine in the home if they are suddenly there all the time.

When it comes to household tasks, you need to make sure there is an equitable division of household duties when you both retire. Don't try to get away with the old "you take care of the inside while I'll take care of the outside routine," because take it from me, that doesn't cut it anymore! (And by the way, the worst move you can make is spending a lot of time playing golf and watching sports in the afternoon, just waiting for your partner to come home from work so she can cook you some dinner. Consider yourself warned!)

Mike was about to get his first post-retirement lesson from the Contessa.

I tend to tease guys a lot for how they act, but the reality is that it is not just men who have a rough time adjusting to retirement; their partners are struggling just as much trying to make sense out of it all. You may have been dreaming for years about the freedom and adventure you'll have when you retire, but it's a huge change to deal with and it can bring a lot of unexpected stress into your life, just when you thought life would be stress-free. As a result, retirement can put enormous amounts of pressure on a marriage and some couples don't survive it.

The Bottom Line

If you are having trouble adjusting to retirement as a couple, don't be shy about getting professional help, and make sure you both attend. Work with your financial advisor or a retirement coach to help clarify the hopes, dreams, and goals you both have so that you can get on the same page and support one another. You will save a lot of time and aggravation and possibly also a partnership by doing this.

At the end of the day, though, retirement is too short to spend it with someone you don't like and who doesn't like you. If you both tried hard and still can't get on the same page, divorce might just be the best answer. It's definitely a better option than unhappiness. And if you thought working in the Corp was bad, living in a tense, unfulfilling relationship for the next twenty to thirty years would be a living hell.

Questions for Self-Reflection
- Are you satisfied with your relationships with your family and friends?
- Do you need more friends?
- How can you improve the quality of your relationships?
- Are some of your relationships starting to slip away from you?
- When was the last time you spoke with your best friend?

- When was the last time you did something fun with a friend?
- When was the last time you spent some quality time with your kids?
- When was the last time you had a meaningful conversation with your kids?
- Do you have meaningful conversations with your spouse?
- Do you feel like your spouse is more of a roommate than a partner?
- How would you rate your marriage?
- How would your partner rate it?
- What are your individual retirement plans?
- What are your retirement plans as a couple?
- Are you aware of your partner's retirement goals, and are they compatible with your own?
- Where do the two of you want to travel?
- Where do you want to live? Where does your partner want to live?
- Is your spouse or partner on board with what you want to do in retirement? If not, what are you going to do about it?

Rating Retirement Principle #1

How would you rate your current relationships on a scale of 1–10 with:

- your partner?
- your kids?
- your friends?

What things can you start doing today to get these ratings to a 10?

Simple Truths

- Loneliness is an emotional problem with a physical consequence that could lead to an early death.
- Many of the relationships developed in your work life die when your work life does.
- There is a very high cost attached to poor communication in any relationship.
- For couples to be happy in retirement, they need to maintain

not just their passion for the marriage but also their individual passion for life.

- Togetherness feels good only when you are doing something you both enjoy.
- If you don't think mattering matters, you're kidding yourself.

5

Retirement Principle #2

Foster Good Health

Take care of your body. It's the only place you have to live.
—*Jim Rohn*

It's hard to enjoy your retirement when you are suffering from poor health. You need to look after yourself so you can enjoy the things you love to do for as long as you can.

Some things to ponder:

- In an August 2017 poll conducted by the Nationwide Retirement Institute, a third of recent retirees said that health problems were interfering with their retirement.
- Out of one hundred healthy sixty-year-old males, thirty-six of them will either suffer a critical illness or die before they turn seventy; and after seventy, the incidence of disease or death climbs exponentially.
- While modern science is keeping us alive longer, it's important to understand that it cannot give us back

our health or vitality past a certain point. You're not always going to be able to run that marathon or climb that mountain.

Many people unthinkingly or even willingly sacrifice their health while they climb the corporate ladder and raise their kids. They end up sitting all day and then when they finally get home, they are too tired to work out and just end up sitting in front of the television. The effects from too many late nights, early meetings, relentless travel, and alcohol- and carb-rich lunches and dinners with clients and colleagues are cumulative and will eventually force you to pay a price. It's not unusual for relatively young people to be taking medication for high blood pressure, for high cholesterol, or to help them sleep at the end of another stressful day.

If we were to chart the health trajectory for the average person from age fifty-five on, it would look something like the one shown in Figure 5.1.

Figure 5.1: The Long Slide into Old Age

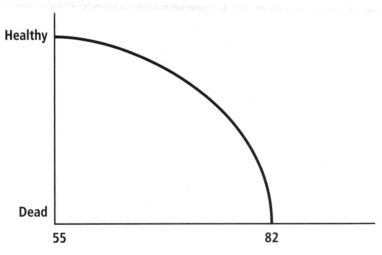

Every year, you will put on a little more weight, with most of that extra weight being fat, and you will have a little less energy. People who follow this pattern are at a higher risk for many kinds of cancer, heart disease, Alzheimer's disease, and premature death.

LESSONS FROM A PANDEMIC

There are countless reasons to keep yourself as healthy as possible for as long as possible, and the COVID-19 crisis only highlighted the importance of staying physically well. Information available at the time of writing clearly pointed to higher risk for severe illness from COVID-19 among older adults and people of any age who had serious underlying medical conditions.

In a study published for the CDC's *Morbidity and Mortality Weekly Report*, researchers found that the majority of patients hospitalized due to COVID-19 had pre-existing conditions (approximately 90% of 1,482 patients from across 14 different states admitted during the period between March 1 and March 30, 2020). The most common underlying conditions were hypertension (49.7%), obesity (48.3%), chronic lung disease (34.6%), diabetes (28.3%) and cardiovascular disease (27.8%).

The takeaway here is that you want to reduce the risk of ending up in a hospital, especially during a pandemic. The good news is that many common pre-existing conditions are reversible through positive lifestyle changes.

Retirement: Your Second Chance at a Healthy Lifestyle

You don't have to follow the path of the average person. Why die younger than you should? Research shows that much of the typical retiree's decline is caused largely by poor lifestyle choices and disuse of both body and mind—the "use it or lose it" principle of aging. Just as retirement is your second chance at living out your dreams and following your passions, so is Victory Lap a second kick at the can for your health. You now have the time to dedicate to exercising and eating right and, with the help of this book, the tools and the motivation to focus on your overall health and well-being to a greater degree than you have in years, or maybe ever.

Stan suddenly realized why he had a craving for sour cream and chives.

If you are willing to take corrective action, instead of getting a little slower, fatter, and weaker each year, you can get fitter, healthier, and stronger. Of course, no one can stop the clock; we can only slow it down. At some point you will inevitably start to decline, but you can improve your chances of delaying that stage and remain in better shape than average until your eighties and beyond. The graph for people adopting this approach is shown in Figure 5.2.

It is better to wear out than rust out.

—Richard Cumberland

Figure 5.2: The Better Way to Age

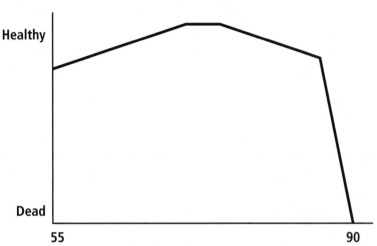

To make this your reality, it comes down to only two primary things: exercising regularly and eating right. This approach is explored in great depth in the book *Younger Next Year* by Chris Crowley and Henry S. Lodge, M.D. It is a must-read for anyone not willing to follow the pattern shown in Figure 5.1. In his book, Dr. Lodge states that over 50 percent of all illnesses common in the last third of your life—heart disease, cancer, stroke, hypertension, diabetes, osteoporosis, and even Alzheimer's disease—can be eliminated through lifestyle changes and that 70 percent of the normal decay associated with aging, such as sore joints and so on, can be delayed and pushed off until near the very end.

There are numerous studies that support the approach taken in *Younger Next Year*, and that's why I'm a loyal follower. For example, in the Dallas Bed Rest and Training Study conducted in 1966, five men in their twenties were asked to spend three weeks resting in bed. Over that short period, they developed many of the physiological characteristics of men twice their age, including higher resting heart rates, higher systolic blood pressure, increased body fat, and a decrease in muscle strength. The men were then put on an eight-week exercise program, which reversed the deterioration brought on by the bed rest.

The same group was tested again thirty years later, and over that period they each had gained fifty pounds, on average, and their average body fat had doubled from 14 percent to 28 percent of body weight. Along with the weight gain, they also experienced a rise in both resting heart rate and blood pressure. Once again, the group was put on an exercise program consisting of walking, jogging, and cycling. After six months, they had lost weight and experienced improvements in resting heart rates and blood pressure, but not to the same extent experienced back in their twenties. There was slippage in performance, although not as much as if they had done nothing.

The takeaway here is that many of the physical changes attributable to aging are in fact caused by disuse. This study clearly showed the risks attached to becoming a couch potato and how quickly physical decline can set in. While the study was done using men, the same holds true for women as well. The truth is that we all can benefit from exercise at any age, and through exercising we will age slower and live healthier, more vigorous lives. I know what I'm going to do. What about you?

The Good News About Exercising

Larry Tucker, a professor of exercise science at Brigham Young University, says that exercisers live significantly longer than sedentary adults, and one way to estimate the extra years exercisers may gain from their physical activity is to measure the length of their telomeres. Telomeres are the protective caps on the end of chromosomes. Long telomeres are related to greater longevity, while shorter ones are related to aging diseases such as cancer and heart disease.

Dr. Tucker conducted a study involving 5,823 US adults and found that men and women who performed high levels of physical activity each week had much longer telomeres than non-exercisers. The adults who worked out on a regular basis had almost nine years less biologic aging compared to those who were sedentary.

Angelique Brellenthin, a research assistant professor in the Department of Kinesiology at Iowa State University and project manager of the CardioRACE Research Trial, states that running is a key lifestyle factor in longevity. She says that runners live on average three years longer than non-runners, and she estimates that "for every one hour you spend running, you net gain an additional seven hours of life. Beyond running, other

> You can't turn back the clock, but you can wind it up again.
>
> —Bonnie Prudden

studies have found that people live on average three to four years longer if they are regularly active compared to inactive." The key is to pick an activity you like and that you can continue doing late in life, such as playing tennis, riding your bike, or walking.

When I train at the pool and gym, I see lots of people older than I am (in their seventies and eighties) who are also fitter than I am. I would love to see some of them do a stress test against the average fifty-year-old. If I could bet on the outcome, I sure could make a lot of easy money—they are that good. They have made healthy living a big part of their lifestyle, and they will reap the returns on that investment for many years to come.

Incorporating an exercise routine into your life is one of the most powerful prescriptions you can write for yourself, and when you make exercise a part of your daily routine it will positively impact every area of your retirement. The health benefits range from the physical to the emotional; from lower cholesterol and blood pressure to decreased stress, improved sleep, and increased optimism, energy, and longevity. In fact, research has shown that exercise can be just as effective as antidepressant drugs for most people. An added bonus is that keeping healthy and eating right will lower the amount of money you'll have to spend on health care as you age, which is one of a retiree's largest expenses.

When you transform your body, another huge benefit is the mental transformation that takes place in sync with the physical changes. Your attitude will improve as you look in the mirror and start to see your body change, especially when you drop those extra pounds you've been carrying around for the longest time. This will lead to other improvements, and the next thing you know, you've quit smoking, cut back on the drinking, and are eating better.

When you feel good, good things tend to happen. Keep working at it and you will feel better in your seventies than you did in your fifties and sixties. And the benefits don't just stop there. Being fit and feeling good will also help you to achieve some of your other retirement goals. If you want to travel, for instance, being physically active will enable you to get to the exotic places you want to visit, and to do so for longer than would otherwise be possible. You may even be able to enjoy more activities with your grandchildren and improve your relationship with your partner.

And if you need or want to continue working in your Victory Lap at least to some degree, being fit and feeling good can help you get a job because you will have more energy and you will feel more confident during the interview. When you feel good about yourself, people notice, and some of them will be the people who will be hiring you. When you do get hired, people will be impressed: the quality of your work will be better than most because you want to be there, you're helpful, you have more physical stamina, and mentally you're at the top of your game. Because your attitude is healthy and you feel positive about things, you will be willing to grow and learn new things.

Healthy Diet: You Are What You Eat

Studies have proven that weight loss and maintaining an ideal weight is 80-percent nutrition and 20-percent exercise. Bet you didn't know that, did you? Your diet matters a lot in the great scheme of things, so if you want to live longer and be happier, you better stop eating "crap" from now on, as Chris Crowley is fond of saying.

I'm not a nutritionist and this is not a health book, so I won't go into detail about what your ideal diet should look like. There are lots of great books out there with advice and recipes for improving your diet. The bottom line is, eat properly: Eat lots of fruits, vegetables, whole grains, and non-fat dairy products. Cut back on salt and processed foods. Keep your caloric consumption down and stay as lean as possible.

One day I read an article in the *Toronto Star* (September 7, 2019) that really drove home the impact nutrition can have on overall health. Entitled "How a fussy eater's diet led to blindness," this article told the story of a teenager from the United Kingdom who had lost his sight after following the same diet for about seven years. Every day his diet consisted of eating fries from the local fish-and-chip shop, Pringles (potato chips that come in a can), white bread, processed ham slices, and sausages.

Eating like this usually results in a person getting fat and having poor cardiovascular health, but in this particular case, it also affected the teen's nervous system, resulting in blindness. The first signs that things were going wrong were that he was feeling tired all the time and then he started to have trouble with his hearing, all caused by his poor diet. This case highlights the importance of eating a varied diet.

Never Stop Learning: Use It or Lose It

When you are working, you are constantly learning new things; but when you retire and don't continue working in some capacity, you need to find new sources for challenging your brain to stay mentally sharp. Some people do it through crossword puzzles and sudoku, but that's not really enough, and there are lots of other ways to stay mentally stimulated and have fun while you're doing it. For example, take an adult-education course at a university or community college to learn something new. Or learn to play a musical instrument or to speak a new language. When you travel, act like a student and be curious about things. Learn something new about the place you are visiting.

> Once you stop learning, you start dying.
> —Albert Einstein

If you focus on keeping your brain challenged by experiencing and learning new things on a regular basis, not only will you slow down and stave off cognitive decline, your brain will continue to flourish, growing better and faster every day.

A study done at the Rush University Medical Center in Chicago tracked 2,765 older adults over a ten-year period. They found that changes in lifestyle—avoiding red meat, taking more walks, doing the Sunday crossword, and sticking to one glass of wine at dinner—could reduce the risk of Alzheimer's by 60 percent. Another study, which was published in 2020 in *Alzheimer's & Dementia: The Journal of the Alzheimer's Association*, found that changes in lifestyle not only stopped cognitive decline in people at risk for Alzheimer's but actually increased their memory and thinking skills within eighteen months.

We are all wired to want to learn, explore, and be creative. Research shows that when we learn and experience new things, we are happier. Learning also keeps your mind sharp and helps you to keep pace with changes in technology. It allows you to discover new passions (scuba diving, anyone?) and meet new people who might turn into friends, and it gives you a sense of personal satisfaction and accomplishment. In the information age and with the help of technology, learning something new has never been easier, so you need to take advantage of that.

My Story

I was on a path similar to the one shown in Figure 5.1 until, thankfully, I woke up and decided to do something about it! Everyone these days is talking about longevity, but personally I am more concerned over quality of life than quantity of life. My focus is on increasing my number of disability-free, healthy years, and compressing the bad stuff into a couple of years at the end, as shown in Figure 5.2.

I want to enjoy my Victory Lap for as long as possible, in a slimmer, healthier body. This goal, constantly in mind, drives what I eat and drink, how much I sleep, and my commitment to daily exercise. I try to incorporate exercise into my daily tasks as much as I can, walking whenever possible and riding my bike to do simple errands. Believe me, it all adds up, and one day I will be able to fit into my old pair of size 36 pants. Can't wait to get there!

If things go according to plan, when I turn seventy I will be noticeably ahead of the average boomer in terms of health and happiness. Even better, this difference will continue to grow larger as time goes on. Not a bad payoff, is it? I also plan on going back to school soon and will be signing up for a marketing course to help with my new business. Who says an old dog can't learn new tricks?

Questions for Self-Reflection
- Do you get regular exercise?
- What does getting fit and healthy mean to you?
- Do you drink too much?
- Do you eat too much?
- Do you watch too much TV or spend too much time on social media?
- Do you have enough intellectual stimulation?
- What three things would you like to learn about?

Rating Retirement Principle #2
How would you rate the following on a scale of 1–10:

- your physical health?
- your mental health?
- your diet?

What can you do today to get these ratings to a 10?

Simple Truths
- In Victory Lap you can stay active and get younger and fitter; or you can passively withdraw into traditional retirement and just get old.
- Exercising and eating right are key anti-aging strategies. They are the magic pill that you have been looking for.
- The more you use your brain, the more you can use your brain.
- Having a lot of money will be of little use if you are not healthy enough to spend it.

6

Retirement Principle #3

Achieve Financial Independence

Retirement is wonderful if you have two essentials—much to live on and much to live for.
—*Author unknown*

Financial independence is a prerequisite for anyone contemplating a transition to Victory Lap. It's the point at which your basic (non-discretionary) living expenses are covered by your passive (non-work) income. In other words, the amount of annual cash flow you require to keep a roof over your head, put food on the table, and pay for the basic necessities (heating, electricity, property taxes, and other essential expenses) can be covered without you having to work to earn an income.

The day you achieve financial independence is the day you no longer need to work in order to survive. If you choose to continue working at this point—be it to give yourself a financial buffer, to finance specific retirement goals, or simply to stay challenged and engaged—then you are working because you *want* to, not because you *have* to. If you are unfamiliar with the idea, we refer you to our first book, *Victory Lap Retirement*, to gain a deeper understanding of this important concept. As for financial planning for retirement, there are lots of excellent books out there to help you with the details, so we won't go into too much depth here. This book focuses on the lifestyle planning piece, but there are some key financial planning points to consider.

To figure out how much money you will need to have saved to consider yourself financially independent and/or to be able to retire, you should have a detailed financial plan created by an accredited financial advisor or financial planner; but by itself that's not enough, because financial planning fails without adequate lifestyle planning. You need to have a good handle on exactly what kind of life you want to live in Victory Lap—what you want to do in retirement and how much it will cost you. Until you do that, you will never be sure you have enough money, and because of that uncertainty, you will always feel the need for a little more.

If you don't have a good handle on how much money you will need in retirement, don't feel bad, because you are not alone. Research has shown that 80 percent of the American public has never taken the time to figure out how much money they'll need to last through retirement and how much they must save. Until you do that, you are just guessing about how much money you will need, and many people guess wrong.

People in the FIRE movement take this financial independence stuff seriously and try to achieve it as early in life as possible. (As I mentioned in the Introduction, FIRE stands for the goal to have financial independence and retire early. I'm a proud member of this community, except I don't believe in the RE part.) They use a general rule of thumb that's common to the financial planning industry to determine when they can quit working, based on achieving a level of savings equivalent to twenty-five times your annual spend rate, net of government pensions and work pensions.

For example, if you believe that you can live comfortably on $60,000 a year, you would deduct from that amount the income you expect to receive from government pensions, say $15,000 annually. Therefore, you would need income of $45,000 from your own investments every year to finance your retirement life-style. And that would require retirement savings of $1,125,000 to maintain your financial independence during retirement ($45,000 x 25 years = $1,125,000).

The rule of thumb is derived from a concept called SWR (sustainable withdrawal rate), which states that a retiree can safely withdraw 4 percent of their retirement investments plus inflation for the rest of their lives. If you have been following along, you will have noticed that the $45,000 you will be drawing out of savings for the first year is 4 percent of the $1,125,000 you hold in retirement savings.

While the FIRE approach works for me, some of you might not be comfortable with it due to the high concentration in equities required to ensure that the 4-percent rule works. At the end of the day, you need to pick an appropriate investing methodology that delivers what you need and lets you sleep at night. Everyone's situation is different and so are people's levels of risk tolerance, comfort with investing, and the cost of the lifestyle they envision for themselves in retirement. The point here is, you need to be very clear about your retirement goals and then put a financial plan in place to support them.

Whether you choose to go the aggressive FIRE route or to retire closer to the traditional retirement age of sixty-five, you still need to get a handle on how you want to live in your Victory Lap, what it will cost, and whether you will have enough income to finance your life beyond work. Many people have a good understanding of the financial side but not so much on the lifestyle cost side. The best way of eliminating uncertainty is to monitor your spending for a year prior to retiring and add in the cost of any extras, such as trips or expensive hobbies, you might want to splurge on in retirement. FIRE or not, when you know exactly how much your annual retirement spend is and you've confirmed that you can stay within the 4-percent withdrawal range, Bob's your uncle.

If by chance your financial plan falls short, you have two options: either cut back on some of your expenses and some of the things you plan to do in retirement, or generate some active income through part-time work.

The Importance of Having a Trusted Advisor

The Contessa was forced to work from home during the COVID-19 pandemic, and I got a chance to see her in action dealing with her clients. One thing I noticed was that, early on when the markets were sharply declining, she wasn't getting a lot of worried calls from her clients wondering what to do. Rather, she was doing most of the calling, making sure her clients were all right and not overly stressed out about things. She had taught them well over the years, and not one client panicked and ran from the market; in fact, many were actively looking for bargains to pick up because, as smart investors know, there is nothing better than a good sale.

It was hard to see the market take a sharp drop like it did during the pandemic. Some people felt like throwing up, watching their hard-earned retirement savings disappear right before their eyes. Without an advisor, they could have panicked and sold out, which would have been the worst thing to do. Watching the Contessa in action got me thinking about how vulnerable some people really are and why, for some people, having the benefit of a trusted advisor makes sense.

Taking risk in the markets can be scary, but erring too far on the other side can be a problem too. Some people make the mistake of being too conservative in their investing, which lowers the returns earned on their portfolio. How your investments perform is what determines your monthly cash flow in retirement, and therefore playing it too safe can cost you large over time.

Retirement is a major life event that needs to be planned for properly. You need to figure out how best to turn your accumulated investments into retirement income, and you need to ensure that income lasts as long as you do. For many people, it makes sense to engage a trusted advisor, be it a financial planner or an investment advisor, when they are close to retiring. It's comforting knowing that you have a trusted advisor in your corner who knows what they are doing, especially during a market meltdown.

A trusted advisor will help you answer the big questions:

1. Are you financially ready to retire? Do you know your number?

2. How should you invest your retirement assets to ensure that you don't outlive your money?
3. When should you apply for Social Security/CPP?
4. How can you fund any unanticipated medical costs?
5. What's the best strategy for withdrawing income from your retirement accounts in order to meet your spending needs and make your money last as long as possible?

As retirement goes on, other key lifestyle questions will appear, such as:

1. Should you sell your house, rent an apartment, or move into a retirement home?
2. Does a reverse mortgage make sense for you?
3. How will you fund higher care costs later in life?

Having a trusted sounding board, someone you can call for advice, is a big help when faced with questions like this, and it will help ensure that you come up with the right answers for you.

One troubling thing I have heard about on more than one occasion from other advisors is that the person responsible for the banking/investing in the family (usually the husband) would get sick and the spouse (usually the wife) would have no clue where anything was or who to talk to. Passwords were missing along with original documentation, and there would be a mad scramble to put everything in order before it was too late. Trying to get a lawyer/investment advisor/banker to attend a hospital room is not always an easy thing to do, especially during a pandemic, and it causes a lot of stress for the surviving spouse and their kids who end up trying to help. Please do not let this happen to you.

Bottom line: If you don't understand investing or retirement planning and have no interest in learning, you should seek the help of a professional who knows this stuff inside and out.

LESSONS FROM A PANDEMIC

When markets crashed with the onset of the COVID-19 pandemic, many retirees and people approaching retirement who thought they were financially prepared were now worried that their life spans might exceed their wealth spans. Although markets rebounded quickly, the dramatic downturn was a tough financial lesson for many investors.

That is why we keep preaching about why it is a good idea to keep generating some level of active income even after you've officially retired, in order to reduce risk and protect against market declines. Look at it this way: if you could generate $10,000 per year in active income, that would be equivalent to withdrawing 4 percent from a $250,000 portfolio; and $20,000 per year in active income would be equivalent to 4 percent of a $500,000 portfolio. Working just a little bit, even part-time, after you've retired from your career means you need to withdraw less from your savings. Instead, you can keep that money invested and working for you and it will go further. It just makes sense to work to some degree in Victory Lap to protect against future market declines, and the possibility that you might live a lot longer than you think.

The pandemic also underscored the value of having financial independence. Some people who needed their work income to survive had to suck it up and go back to work in risky environments (for example, in a meat-packing plant that was riddled with COVID-19). How sad was that? The fortunate ones—the ones who had achieved financial independence—had the power to put their health first and say no.

My Story

Today in Victory Lap I have a different attitude toward money, and it's changed the way I behave. Before, I focused on money and saving for retirement a lot. I would read countless business publications and books on personal finance. I also spent a lot of time watching business shows on TV and following daily stock market prices numerous times throughout the day on my phone.

Today, thankfully, I rarely check my portfolio and I honestly couldn't tell you how much I have because I haven't looked in a while. The reason I don't look is that I have a financial advisor now who looks after that and, even better, my advisor also happens to be my wife, the Contessa.

I handed control of my investment portfolio over to her once I got clear on what the cost of my desired Victory Lap lifestyle would be and then confirmed that I had sufficient cash flow to fund that lifestyle. Now I can live without spending time worrying about money. And that is a special feeling, let me tell you!

I have achieved a level of financial independence where my basic living expenses are covered by income from government pensions and from drawing down the financial assets I have managed to accumulate over the years at a sustainable rate. My other discretionary lifestyle expenses—gym membership, vacation trips, entertainment, and so on—are covered by my fun money. That's the extra money I earn during my Victory Lap by doing part-time work that I love and am passionate about. I'm not going to run out of money, and I no longer worry about how much dinner at a nice restaurant will cost. I'm able to live a comfortable life based on my spending goals, so why worry?

Questions for Self-Reflection
- Have you achieved financial independence?
- Do you have a financial plan?

- Do you have a lifestyle plan?
- Are you satisfied with your financial planning for retirement?
- How much money do you need to live on annually in retirement?
- How much passive income will you have coming in annually?
- Do you need to work part-time to maintain your standard of living in retirement?
- Can you sleep at night, or are you kept awake by fears of outliving your money?

Rating Retirement Principle #3

How would you rate the following on a scale of 1–10:

- your lifestyle planning?
- your financial planning?
- how close you are to being financially independent?

What things can you start doing today to get these ratings to a 10?

Simple Truths

- Retirement happiness doesn't have to cost much.
- Most people don't know how they want to live in retirement.
- Once you know you have enough by knowing exactly how much your Victory Lap lifestyle will cost you, you will never have to worry about money again.
- Working longer reduces the risk of market declines and of not having enough money.
- The longer you work in Victory Lap, the higher your standard of living can be.
- Just because you have a lot of money doesn't guarantee that you are going to be happy in retirement.

7

Retirement Principle #4

Reignite Your Sense of Adventure

Twenty years from now you will be more disappointed by the things you didn't do than by the ones you did do. So throw off the bowlines. Sail away from the safe harbor. Catch the trade winds in your sails. Explore. Dream. Discover.
—*Mark Twain*

As kids we are curious about things, but as we get older, we tend to replace curiosity with certainty and avoid venturing far from our comfort zone so we won't get hurt. To enjoy a great retirement, we need to regain the spontaneity of childhood and enjoy each day of our lives, just like when we were kids. Remember how it felt being a child and not being scared to try something new? Remember how we used to do things just because they were fun? Victory Lap is your time to get curious again about the world around you; a time to explore new possibilities and aspire to more fulfilling experiences—or peak experiences, as we like to call them.

Continuing to grow is crucial to your well-being. So, our advice to you is to fill your retirement with as many adventures and peak experiences as possible while you still can. Establish some values-based goals that will stretch you mentally and physically past your current limits (more on how to do this in parts 3 and 4). Such goals could include things like walking the Camino de Santiago in Spain, starting a new business, going back to school, or travelling to an exotic place. Read books about somewhere in the world you have never been, and then plan on going there. Before going, learn about the people—their history, their language, their culture and traditions—and while there, try their favorite foods.

Because of the internet, it's easy to create as many adventures as you want. The world really is at our fingertips and we need to take advantage of that. There is no better time than during your Victory Lap to discover new places and experience new things. And if you don't want to travel, you can experience a sense of adventure by learning a new technology, how to play the guitar, or how to golf, right here at home. Perhaps explore some of the things your grandkids are interested in. Or it can be as simple as exercising more and making new friends—anything that will expose you to new experiences and push you out of your comfort zone.

LESSONS FROM A PANDEMIC

During the COVID-19 crisis, we couldn't go on road trips or adventures even farther away because of the pandemic travel restrictions (although such trips would have been more affordable when the price of gas was cheap). But that didn't stop us, because there was still a lot we could do while we self-isolated at home. Many of us used our computers to learn new things and to do research on future trips we planned to go on. It was a good time to prepare for future adventures and catch up on learning about new technology.

Looking for some new challenging adventures? Here are some ideas:

- Take an educational vacation adventure.
- Rent an RV and visit a national park.
- Go to a bike training camp in France.
- Learn to scuba dive in Mexico.
- Take a cooking class.
- Start a blog.
- Write a book.
- Climb a mountain.
- Learn to play pickle ball.

You will enjoy your adventures far more than buying more stuff you don't need. In fact, there is research that shows spending money on experiences rather than things can provide a person with more happiness. Also, new experiences will form new memories and become part of your identity. Take it from me, your adventures and experiences will continue to bring fulfillment and stimulate good memories long after you have gone to Goodwill to drop off the stuff you bought and didn't need.

Please Don't Whine That You Don't Have the Money

Of course, some of the goals you set for yourself in Victory Lap will cost money, and sometimes lots of it. That's why it's so important to do your lifestyle planning first, before you go into too much detail in your financial planning. As we discussed in the previous chapter, you need to ensure that you will have enough assets to cover all the peak experiences you want to have, and enough income in retirement to sustain the lifestyle you envision for yourself. But you may also be pleasantly surprised, like I was, to discover that many of the things you want to do don't require a lot of money.

Sure, to afford the life you want in Victory Lap you might need to get a part-time job and cut back on some expenses (like purchasing that pair of designer jeans or a set of new golf clubs) so you can go on that trip to Cuba you've always been dreaming about. Or, instead of buying that fancy new couch for the living room that you will never use, why not take that trip to New York City, eat breakfast at Tiffany's, and stay at the Waldorf? It's all about knowing what you want and then doing what it takes to achieve those goals. It's about your priorities at this stage in your life and making trade-offs and adjustments so you can do the things that really matter to you.

Saving up for a peak experience will give you something to get excited about and give you rich memories for a lifetime, and you don't have to go around the world to enjoy some peak experiences. Within one hundred miles of your home there are probably a lot of places you have never been, filled with things that will amaze and excite you. Canada and the United States are big countries that a person could spend a lifetime exploring, so why not have at it?

Learning to Fly Again

At my retirement presentations I always tell the story of Ria and her first plane ride. Ria is a seventy-nine-year-old grandmother who lives in the Netherlands, and until recently she had never been on a plane. Her husband was afraid of heights, which meant that traveling on a plane was out of the question for them both. When he passed away a couple of years ago, Ria decided that flying was something she had to do, as she didn't want to have that as a regret in life, and so she put a plan together to make it happen.

She talked her granddaughter into going with her to the local amusement park so she could train on the roller coaster, and if you google "Ria's first plane ride" you can see what actually happened. The sound of her laughing like a child on that roller

Vasilyev Alexandr/Shutterstock.com

coaster always makes me smile and, even better, Ria did finally take that first plane ride soon after. Ria serves as a reminder to us all that you are never too old to face your fears and never too old to learn and experience new things.

Because we have the benefit of having both a little money and time when we hit retirement, we can finally switch back from "survival mode" to "adventure mode." We can start having fun again like Ria, feeling excited like a kid again and not being afraid of attempting new things. Just think about all the roads untraveled; the untapped potential within you; all the life you still have to live. What is it you've always wanted to do?

My Story

When I was dragging myself out of Retirement Hell, I needed to get my sense of adventure back and I knew the best way of doing that was to book a trip to Disney World for the Contessa and me. Visiting Disney was magical to me: it was like releasing a genie from the bottle. It rekindled the imagination and creativity in me, and it got me excited about all the things I wanted to try and do in the years ahead. Well worth the price of admission, I would say.

Today, my goals include doing presentations on Victory Lap Retirement in different parts of the world. I want to learn Spanish and how to play the guitar. I want to learn how to ballroom dance so I can dance at weddings instead of sitting on a chair. I want to go on safari in South Africa and travel in a hot-air balloon over a game preserve with the Contessa. I want to visit my son in Australia and go in a shark cage and get face-to-face with a great white. And that's only the tip of the iceberg!

People think I must have a lot of money in the bank to go on all the adventures I do, but the truth is, I don't. I earn everything that I spend on my adventures through the work I continue to do (and love) in my Victory Lap. The fun money I earn is what I use to fund my peak experiences. I don't always have enough to afford to stay in the best of places, but that's OK because I'm willing to do whatever it takes to make the adventure happen. And that's why you won't see me wasting money on designer clothing or buying fancy cars; it's so I can afford to do the things I want to do in retirement.

I've learned that you don't need a lot of money to enjoy a great retirement. You just need to be curious, have a sense of adventure, and be resourceful so you can do what it takes. I've traveled the world and learned an important lesson from people less fortunate than me: it doesn't take a lot of money to be happy.

Questions for Self-Reflection
- Have you started planning for some of the peak experiences you want to have in your Victory Lap?
- What new leisure activities would you like to try?
- What new adventures do you want to go on, and with whom?
- What activities get you excited?
- When was the last time you felt really alive?

Rating Retirement Principle #4

How would you rate your level of exposure to new adventures and experiences on a scale of 1–10? What things can you start doing today to get that rating to a 10?

Simple Truths

- You need to find opportunities that allow you to keep growing and improving because it's growth and being tested that generates happiness.
- Life is either a daring adventure or boring.
- If you think adventure is dangerous, try living a boring retirement. Playing it safe is a gamble too.
- Sadly, many retirees wake up too late to the fact that they have forgotten how to have fun.
- Some of the best things in retirement aren't things.

8

Retirement Principle #5

Tap into Your Spirituality

Happiness cannot be traveled to, owned, earned or worn. It is the spiritual experience of living every minute with love, grace and gratitude.
—Denis Waitley

O ne of the keys to a happy, healthy, and fulfilling retirement is learning (or relearning) to tap into your spiritual side. Spirituality comes in many different forms, and you don't need to go to a church, synagogue, mosque, or other places of worship to be spiritual. You can also find spiritual nourishment in solitude, through meditation, through the practice of yoga, or in nature. Do whatever works for you.

Religious Communities

People of faith tend to be more resilient to life's challenges, and because of this, they generally are less stressed and are on average healthier and happier. Having a sense that you're not in the world alone and that you are connected with others and part of something much bigger than yourself, brings healing and provides resiliency, solace, purpose, and hope. This is true whatever stage you are at in life, but these benefits can be especially helpful in retirement, when you no longer have the daily collegiality and social aspect of your work community.

A number of studies have shown that people who belong to a faith-based community benefit from increased longevity. One study done by Baldwin Way, a psychology professor at Ohio State University, concluded that churchgoers can expect to live up to nine years longer than people who do not belong to a faith-based community. A 2017 study published in *PLOS One* found that regular attendance at religious services is linked to reductions in the body's stress responses, resulting in worshippers being 55-percent less likely to die during the follow-up period of up to eighteen years.

In addition to promoting longevity, being a part of a religious community also helps to improve one's quality of life. It does so by alleviating the dangers of isolation and loneliness (Retirement Principle #1) because you're part of a supportive community. It brings like-minded people together to do good things for themselves and for others (Retirement Principle #7), and the payoff is that they have purpose (Retirement Principle #9) and they feel connected to something bigger than themselves.

If you are not into organized religion, there are other ways to achieve the same positive effects. Individual prayer triggers the relaxation response, a state of mind–body rest that has been shown to decrease stress, heart rate, and blood pressure. These are the same benefits that people derive from practicing meditation and yoga.

Meditation, Mindfulness, and Yoga

Thousands of studies have highlighted the many benefits of yoga and meditation. Yoga is more of a physical practice, but it also has a meditative and spiritual grounding that helps keep the mind sharp, relieves a person's stress levels, and improves overall well-being. All forms of meditation and mindfulness improve mental focus and an overall feeling of being uplifted emotionally due to deep relaxation. The more you meditate or practice mindfulness or yoga, the better you become at handling stress, allowing you to react better to what is happening to you in a more calm and relaxed manner.

Communing with Nature

Most of us spend the bulk of our time working in offices only to, at the end of the day, go home and spend the rest of our time in front of the TV and/or computer. In fact, in 2001, a survey sponsored by the U.S. Environmental Protection Agency found that, on average, Americans spend 87 percent of their time indoors and 6 percent in an enclosed vehicle, which is not a good thing. A lifestyle devoid of being outside in nature makes it challenging to get in tune with your spirituality.

Spending time in nature by taking a walk in the woods, taking a boat ride, or simply sitting on the dock at the cottage reading a book will rejuvenate your spirit, give you a more positive outlook on life, and improve your health and happiness big-time. It's an easy way to improve physical and mental health and has been credited with reducing blood pressure and stress as well as improving mental health, cognitive abilities, and sleep patterns.

And if you need more convincing about the benefits of spending time in nature, Qing Li, a professor at the Nippon Medical School in Tokyo, found that when people walk or stay overnight in forests they often exhibit changes in the blood that are associated with protection against cancer, better immunity, and lower blood pressure. Dr. Li's research found that when people walk through a forest, they inhale phytoncides that increase their number of natural killer (NK) cells, which supports the immune system and is associated with a lower risk of cancer. And in a 2010 study, another group of Japanese researchers found that people who took two long walks through forests on consecutive days increased their NK cells by 50 percent and the activity of those cells by 56 percent; futhermore, the cells' activity levels remained 23-percent higher than usual for the month following the walks.

In North America we have the benefit of numerous easily accessible parks and natural spaces that have plenty of walking and riding trails. We have no excuses for not spending more time outside enjoying the free gift that Mother Nature has kindly given us. Walking in nature is great therapy: it's rejuvenating, and it will do more to relieve your stress and recharge you than taking marijuana or other drugs, having three martinis, or binge-watching *Game of Thrones*. And it won't cost you a penny.

My Story

The George River is my go-to place for practicing my spirituality and finding perspective. It's the one place where I can escape from stress and technology because, thankfully, nothing works up there, and the only things you can do are eat, sleep, fish, and think.

Whenever I go there, I get this feeling of being connected to something "bigger" than me. The river has a way of opening up my mind, and it was there that I came up with my theory about the important connection between work, retirement, and our innate needs.

Mike gets his spiritual nourishment fly fishing at the George.

One day while sitting on a rock by the river, I started thinking about salmon and their life cycle. They are born in the river and then, after a period of time, they migrate and venture out into the ocean for the next four years. They spend that time feeding and trying to escape other predators who want to eat them, the worst being humans with their fishing nets. What is amazing to me is that after four years of struggling to survive and traveling thousands of miles in the ocean, salmon have the ability to return to the same river they were born in, sometimes to the same exact spot, so they can spawn in order to keep the species going. No one tells the salmon what to do or when to do it. It's an instinctual need—one they are born with and can't opt out of.

I believe life works the same way for us, and that we are all born with a sense of mission that lies dormant within us. After spending our initial years being educated (in the river) we are thrown out into the working world (the ocean) and struggle to survive/thrive for the next thirty-plus years. This struggle comes at a significant cost as the stress we encounter disconnects us from the natural world, our family, and even ourselves. At some point we gain financial independence and get our freedom back. We start thinking about retiring, and this triggers our innate needs to kick in again, similar to what happens to the salmon when they feel the urge to start making their way back to the river they were born in.

Sometimes when they return, the salmon are blocked from going upriver because someone decided to build a hydro dam across the river, and this causes the salmon a lot of stress as they try to get past the dam. Some of the lucky ones figure out a way to get past the dam via the fish ladder and continue upriver; but others won't find it, and as a result will never get to complete their mission.

When we retire, many of us start to feel a need to complete our mission so that we can satisfy that empty feeling inside us, but some face the obstacle (the hydro dam) of still not knowing what our mission is. What is it that we were meant to do? What makes us feel fulfilled? How can we use the special talents that we were given?

I believe our mission is about finding significance and connectedness through what we can give; it's about caring for and helping others. Perhaps this is why so many retirees feel the need to volunteer in retirement. Not only can practicing spirituality in some form help to give you the meaning and connectedness you seek at this time in your life, it can also allow you to open up the mental and emotional space necessary to discover your own personal mission.

You transcend to something greater when your thinking shifts from what you can get for yourself to how you can serve others; from everything being all about you to it being about community, belonging, and feeling a part of something much bigger. The way we think about things changes when we tap into our spiritual selves: winning doesn't matter anymore, we don't need to prove ourselves anymore, materialistic things don't matter anymore—our ego thankfully has finally left the building.

When you find a way to be part of a community and to give back, helping others in need, you change from a taker to a giver. I believe that is our mission, and embracing spirituality offers us a way to discover it and fulfill it; as a result, we experience a new, deeper level of significance and the hunger goes away. What a master plan!

LESSONS FROM A PANDEMIC

The pandemic highlighted the importance of having faith and hope and of being connected to others. People of faith coped with the pandemic better than many others, as being part of a community is very supportive and healing. Although they couldn't gather together physically, faith communities of all kinds were able to connect virtually. This gave them a sense of togetherness and support; they knew they were not alone. As a result, they were less stressed and more resilient than some others.

And there was a moment that brought us all together, no matter how you choose to practice your spirituality. On Easter Sunday, Andrea Bocelli performed a concert called *Music for Hope* from the Duomo cathedral in Milan. There was no audience present, in keeping with COVID-19 restrictions. For his last song, Bocelli, who is blind, walked outside the church unaided and sang "Amazing Grace." It was very powerful—the song made all the more poignant by the scenes they showed of deserted streets from various cities around the globe. It made us feel connected to everyone else in the world, like we were all in it together, and that together we would find a way out.

If you were able to hear that song and watch those images without shedding a tear, you were much stronger than me!

Questions for Self-Reflection
- How do you practice your spirituality?
- Where do you go to practice it?
- When was the last time you practiced it? How did it make you feel?
- When was the last time you went for a walk in nature?
- How are you going to complete your mission?

Rating Retirement Principle #5
How would you rate your spiritual life on a scale of 1–10? What can you do to get the rating to a 10?

Simple Truths
- Practicing spirituality increases resiliency and provides you with a sense of perspective and meaning.
- Spirituality helps you deal with the ups and downs of everyday life.
- There is strength in belonging to a group of people who share similar beliefs and values.
- Meditation is about waking up to who you really are and giving thanks for what you have.
- Happy retirees have faith and hope and gratitude for the way things are.

9

Retirement Principle #6

Find Your Tribes

Surround yourself with people who add value to your life. Who challenge you to be greater than you were yesterday. Who sprinkle magic into your existence, just like you do to theirs. Life isn't to be done alone. Find your tribe and journey freely and loyally together.
    —Alex Elle

One commonly experienced negative aspect of leaving your career is missing the camaraderie you enjoyed while at work. In order to be happy and avoid loneliness, it's important that you come up with a suitable replacement. A great way to connect with others is to join a tribe—a group of people who think like you and are passionate about the same things as you.

Similar to religious communities (Retirement Principle #5), tribes serve as mutual support networks that help offset loneliness (Retirement Principle #1), a lack of purpose (Retirement Principle #9), and a sedentary lifestyle (Retirement Principle #2), which could all shorten life expectancy and certainly reduce the quality of your life in retirement.

The significant health benefit attached to belonging to a tribe was demonstrated in a large study by Julianne Holt-Lunstad of Brigham Young University, which found that people with greater social connection had a 50-percent lower risk of early death. OK, so where do I sign up?

Have an Active Social Network

There are all kinds of tribes you can join; which one(s) you align yourself with just depends on what you enjoy doing and what you are looking for. A good place to start is to check out your local community guide. Find out where people who have a similar interest to you hang out. Are there courses or seminars you could attend? Are there Facebook groups or online forums you could join?

If your passion is dancing, sign up for a dance class at the local recreation center. If your passion is investing, join an investing club. If you want to give back to the community, join a service club. If you love singing, find a choir to join. If you love reading, take a university or college course or join a book club. The same goes for photography, cooking, tennis—just about any interest you can think of. Spending time around people who are already doing what you want to do, people who you have a personal connection with, and who support, what you are trying to accomplish, is one of the fastest ways to achieve success.

Joining a tribe will make you feel good, because you are part of a common cause and the rest of the group will challenge you to be better than you were yesterday, plus you will have a great time hanging out with great people. Tribes serve to broaden your social network, and they also give you and your partner some time and space to pursue your individual passions and interests.

People like Weed Woman and Window Guy (remember them from Chapter 1?) would benefit greatly from finding a suitable tribe. They wouldn't feel lonely or isolated anymore, and being part of a tribe would give them something to do when the cold weather arrives and they can't work outside anymore.

My Story

After starting my Victory Lap, I joined a Masters swim class at the local community pool. We swim three times a week, and on the first Monday of each month, we go out for beers and have an opportunity to talk and share our stories.

In the faster lane beside mine is a Retirement Rebel who is over eighty years old and he is just killing it (or maybe he's killing me). Every time I get passed by him, I laugh, knowing what is possible if I'm willing to do the work.

In addition to my swim tribe, I also joined Toastmasters and a Facebook group called "Younger Next Year." These tribes are filled with people who have done, or are trying to do, what I want to do in different areas of my life. I like hanging around my tribes because it allows me to connect with people who have interests and beliefs similar to mine, and we share a common goal of improving the quality of our remaining years. Hanging around them helps motivate me to show up and achieve my goals. They hold me accountable and show me what's possible if I'm willing to put the work in.

Questions for Self-Reflection
- What groups would you like to join?
- Why haven't you joined?
- How much time do you spend with people who inspire you?
- What would you like to learn?
- What would you like to accomplish?

Rating Retirement Principle #6

How would you rate your level of involvement with tribes on a scale of 1–10? What things can you start doing today to get the rating to a 10?

Simple Truths

- Life isn't to be done alone; find your tribes.
- Our chosen tribes will show us what we are capable of.
- There is nothing better than to be on a shared mission with people you respect and care about.
- Joining a tribe will give you some necessary alone time from your partner and allow you to enjoy something that maybe your partner doesn't.
- Joining tribes who share your beliefs, values, and sense of purpose can help you achieve your goals more quickly.

10

Retirement Principle #7

Make the Most of Your Time

All of us are on borrowed time. There are no refunds and there are no guarantees. At some point, the only time you'll have to worry about is the time you've wasted.
—Seth Godin (blog)

Retirement is our last kick at the can—because it's hard to enjoy life when you're six feet under. With this in mind, you need to start using your remaining time wisely and refuse to waste it on things that don't matter. The beauty of being in your Victory Lap is that you are given the gift of an extra two thousand hours a year, previously spent at work, to do with as you please. You no longer have any excuses for why you can't do the things you need or want to do. The trick to a fulfilling retirement is to plan ahead to invest those hours doing meaningful things.

A Long Life vs. a Good Life

By adopting the nine retirement principles, odds are good that you will have decades of living ahead of you, but does a longer life really matter if the extra time you gain sucks? It would be such a waste to spend your extra time doing nothing, being bored, and complaining about it all the time. The goal here isn't just to add years to your life; it's all about adding quality life to those extra years.

The smart ones among us will use that time and the nine retirement principles to create the retirement lifestyle they always dreamed about. They know the direction they want their retirement to take, and they focus on the things that will bring happiness and fulfillment. They want this period of their lives to be one of growth and development, not one filled with boredom and regret. Remember, we're going for Retirement Heaven here, not Retirement Hell.

LESSONS FROM A PANDEMIC

The COVID-19 pandemic taught people who couldn't work from home how boring retirement must be when you have more free time than you know what to do with. Before the pandemic, people complained about not having enough time to do things, and then many of them quickly had too much time on their hands. Sounds a lot like Retirement Hell to me.

During the self-isolation and enforced downtime of the pandemic, time slowed to a crawl for those who suddenly couldn't work. The days became a blur; you had trouble remembering what day it was because it didn't matter. Every day was similar to the next: watching news of the virus on TV and making calls to the family to see how they were doing. Without a plan for how to use your time, this is how dull your retirement could be too.

Time Is Something You Can Never Get Back

We should remember that we all have an expiration date and that our retirement time is finite. We only get the next hour once, and then it's gone forever. So, choices about how you spend or invest your retirement time come with real opportunity costs. Next week, the time you spend watching Netflix or being on social media won't matter much in the long run. But if you invest that time creating new memories or learning something new, you will remember it forever.

The opportunity cost of time is the key to making decisions in retirement. Once you know the value of the alternatives you're giving up, you can be smarter about what you're choosing to do. Successful retirees know that time is more valuable than money and that, unlike money, time cannot be replaced when it's gone. They realize that when you're dead, you're dead, and you only get today once. That's why they are so protective of the clock and make every minute count.

Time Exercise

I find it interesting that many of us spend all our working life saving for retirement but give little thought to what we'll invest that money and free time in once we get there. Each week, we all have 168 hours at our disposal. We spend a whole chunk of those sleeping, but we have control over how we spend the remaining sixteen hours left in our day (that's 112 hours per week).

An interesting exercise to do when you're completing your daily journal is to keep track of how you spent your time over the course of an average week. Make sure you record everything, including the time spent watching TV, in front of the computer, on social media, playing video games, and on your smartphone. You might be as surprised by your results as I was by mine. The point is not to feel guilty about having wasted time on empty activities but to learn from the patterns you begin to see and use the data as motivation to spend your time in more meaningful, fulfilling ways.

ROTI: Return on Time Invested

The whole idea of the Time Exercise is to train yourself to invest your time in high-return areas—activities that you enjoy, that you can share with others you love, that will make great new memories, that will help other people, that will help you fulfill your mission—and cut back on low-return activities.

High-return activities include the following:

- spending more time with family and friends
- making new friends
- socializing
- working out regularly
- eating properly
- doing fun things
- traveling
- being outdoors
- learning new things
- helping others
- spending time with your tribes
- setting challenging goals
- cultivating spirituality
- expressing gratitude
- engaging in your art (something we will discuss in greater detail in Chapter 15)

Cutting back on low-return activities, like those listed below, will free up time that can be better invested into the big things that count.

- watching mindless TV
- surfing the internet
- being on social media
- worrying about things beyond your control

Look for ways to simplify your life in retirement. For example, selling things you rarely use can help you gain time for high-return activities as well as provide you with additional capital to finance them. Possibly the most significant example is downsizing from a bigger home than you need, which can free up time that you used to spend maintaining and managing a larger property—and it will also free up capital that can be used to fund your chosen Victory Lap lifestyle.

Understand That Not All Time Is Equal

In retirement there is an important relationship between time and a person's energy and activity levels; in other words, we will all slow down at some point as we age. The quality of our remaining time will inevitably decrease, and we will not be physically able to do some of the things we took for granted before, like swimming across the lake at the cottage.

By now you know you can slow the aging process down by following the retirement principles, but at some point, it will kick in even for us. You need to be aware of this and, like they say, "make hay while the sun is shining"—the sooner the better. Do everything with a sense of purpose and urgency. Take that bike trip in Spain you've been dreaming about; visit your friends in Australia; learn to scuba dive now while you still can. And if you need to work part-time, do it now, so that you can afford to do all the fun things you have on your dance card while you are able to do them.

As you age, those long plane rides you used to take will at some point become intolerable. Your retirement world will start to shrink and you'll spend more time closer to home, spending time with friends and family and doing fun things with your chosen tribes. The trips you do take will become shorter. As a consequence, you will be spending less money as your energy levels go down and your health begins to decline. Which brings us to another important point.

The reality is that the state of your health could change in an instant rather than go into a slow decline, so don't take it for granted. The biggest mistake you can make is putting things off due to being scared about running out of money; because when you are finally confident that you have enough, you may not be physically able to do the things you always wanted to do. Avoid this regret and don't hang on to your money; spend it when you can best enjoy it. Of course, you must be prudent and live within your means, but having a lot of money in your bank account is not going to do you a lot of good when you physically cannot get out of bed.

My Story

My appreciation for time changed during my visits with my mother at the nursing home. Those visits gave me a ton of perspective, and I now look at every sunrise, sunset, and everything in between as a gift—a gift I'm not willing to waste. I now live with a sense of urgency and am focused on doing the things that are important to me—the things that will make me happy today. Because who knows what may happen tomorrow?

My priority every day is to invest my remaining time into my family and friendships, a stable marriage, my health, and work that I enjoy. I refuse to waste precious time doing things I don't enjoy, worrying about things beyond my control, or being mad about something I saw on TV. I've also learned firsthand that it's a mistake to buy things we really don't need that make our lives complicated and force us to waste precious time and money doing unnecessary maintenance.

A perfect example is the hot tub I purchased a few years ago. At the time, I thought it was a good idea. I had visions of it healing my sore muscles after my workouts, and the thought of feeling relief from the warm water kept filling my mind. But it didn't work out that way, and I only used it once this year but still had to clean it weekly and pay for those costly chemicals. It also costs me $400 dollars in the spring and fall for someone to come in and do an opening and closing. Every time I look at it, I feel really stupid, and it's not fun feeling like that, so please don't let something like that happen to you. (I could also tell you about the rowing machine I bought, but that's another story!)

If you have non-essential stuff in your life, getting rid of it will reduce stress and free up time and money that can be invested in the good stuff, like visiting friends and family, traveling, fishing, and working at your art. Or, better yet, avoid buying non-essential stuff in the first place.

Today I'm also very careful about the time I spend on traditional and social media. I used to be addicted to following the stock market, watching the Business News Network, checking stuff out on my phone, and checking for emails. What a waste of life and time! Why did I monitor the markets so compulsively? Why did I let stock prices ruin my day and get my stress up? I wasn't going to sell my stock anyway! It was a complete loss of energy and time and it generated a lot of stress to boot, stress that I didn't want or need. I'm happy to say I no longer do any of that, and only invest my time in things that will give me a good return on that priceless resource.

Questions for Self-Reflection
- What did you learn from doing the Time Exercise?
- What do you waste your time doing?
- What are you spending most of your time on?
- Where do you need to invest more time?
- How much quality time do you spend with your family and friends?
- How much time do you spend working out?
- Are you spending most of your time on things you love?
- If the doctor said you had cancer and only ten years to live, how would you spend your remaining time?
- If the doctor said you had only one more day to live, what regrets would you have? Maybe you should spend some time eliminating those regrets while you still have the chance.

Rating Retirement Principle #7
How would you rate how you are currently investing your time on a scale of 1–10? What things can you start doing today to get the rating to a 10?

Simple Truths
- Every day matters. You need to prioritize what's most important to you with the time you have left.
- Time is too precious to spend it doing something you hate.
- What you decide to do with your time will have big implications on the quality of retirement you will have.
- The best investment you can make is putting more time into your family and relationships.
- You don't have as much time as you think you do.

11

Retirement Principle #8

Adopt the Right Attitude

You can't help getting older, but you don't have to get old.
—George Burns

Did you know that positive people live longer? A study done at Yale University (*YaleNews*, July 29, 2002) found that a positive attitude can extend your life span by seven and a half years, which is more than the longevity gained from low blood pressure, low cholesterol, maintaining a healthy weight, being a non-smoker, or exercising regularly.

If you need more proof about the benefit attached to having a positive attitude, a thirty-year study of 447 people at the Mayo Clinic (*Science Daily*, August 2002) found that optimists had around a 50-percent lower risk of premature death than pessimists.

And if that's still not enough, a Dutch study of 999 people (*JAMA Psychiatry Science*, November 2004) examined the attitudes and longevity of a group of people over the age of sixty-five and reported a "protective relationship" between optimism and mortality. Their conclusion? People with a positive attitude lived longer and were found to have a 77-percent lower risk of heart disease than pessimists.

Why Do Positive People Live Longer?

The answer is that they are better able to handle the stress we as humans are constantly exposed to. A person with a negative attitude has a hard time coping when retirement goes off the rails (as it often does!), and so they get angry and frustrated. They believe that there is nothing they can do to change their future, that tomorrow will be just like today, and that today sucks. The resulting stress from all the negativity causes inflammation, which leads to other health problems which, combined, speed up aging.

A positive retiree, on the other hand, doesn't get as stressed dealing with everyday life and has hope for the future. Less stress means less inflammation and lower blood pressure, which means you end up living longer. Makes sense when you think about it. When you have a positive, optimistic attitude toward retirement, you will be more motivated to challenge yourself, take some risks, and act on the opportunities that will inevitably show up at your door.

Make Gratitude a Habit

A successful Victory Lap Retirement is all about gratitude. It's about appreciating the good things in your life as well as the problems you don't have. If you need some help with that, go visit the nearest hospital ER or volunteer at the local soup kitchen or homeless shelter for some perspective on how small your problems really are compared with other people, and after these visits, you will realize that your life is not as bad as it sometimes seems.

If you watch the news, you will realize that, for most of us, our own problems are pretty insignificant compared to the rest of the world's. For example, how would you like to live in a country like North Korea where you have no freedom at all? Or being forced to work at some god-awful job just so you can put food on the table and pay the rent. Take the time to notice others around you, and you will see lots of people with problems worse than yours.

More importantly, focus on being happy with what you have. We own so much stuff, yet for some reason we have a hard time appreciating it. Perhaps because that's not what we should be truly thankful for anyway. Give thanks for your family, your health, the roof over your head and all the other things you are fortunate to have. Make sure you make a routine of counting your blessings every day and make a practice of recording them in your journal at the end of the day. It will help you keep everything in perspective and ground you during tough times.

> He is a wise man who does not grieve for the things which he has not, but rejoices for those which he has.
>
> —Epictetus

Time to Ditch the Ego

Some retirees have trouble letting go of their ego, as it was their only way of proving their worth to others. Many years of working for the Corp reinforced the need for competition, power, and getting ahead by beating others. With this mind-set, not only is your identity built around work; as a result, your whole idea of self-worth is at the expense of others. People who have been conditioned like this tend to have an unhealthy attitude of putting themselves first, they will never be happy with what they have, and they will always be jealous about what others have. Talk about being in Retirement Hell! In Victory Lap we can fix things by becoming egoless, humble, and satisfied with what we already have. When you are egoless, the stress is gone and you don't feel you have to win anymore.

The Power of Belief: The Placebo Effect

The power of positive thinking is so strong that it can improve not only your outlook but also your physical health. Some studies suggest that as much as 60 to 90 percent of drugs and other therapies prescribed by physicians depend on the placebo effect and what a patient believes for their effectiveness.

The strength of the placebo effect was demonstrated in a study published in the *Annals of Internal Medicine* in 2006 that involved 1,007 patients with severe arthritis in their knees. One group was given "real" acupuncture therapy while another group was given "fake" acupuncture. At the end of the study, an improvement was observed in 53 percent of the patients in the real-acupuncture group versus 51 percent in the simulated-acupuncture group, proving that fake acupuncture was just as effective as real acupuncture due to the placebo effect.

Seems crazy, and we are not done yet. A 2007 study by Erin M. Shackell and Lionel G. Standing at Bishop's University found that just *thinking* about doing an exercise produced nearly identical gains in strength and fitness as actually *doing* the exercise. The study measured the strength gains in three different groups of people. The first group just followed their regular workout routine. The second group was put through two weeks of highly focused strength training, three times a week. The third group listened to audio CDs that had them imagining themselves going through the same workout as the second group.

The results from this study were amazing (and also a bit scary if you happen to own a gym). The first group, which just did what they always did, saw no gains in strength. The second group, which did the specialized workouts, experienced a 28-percent gain in strength. And the third group, which did not physically exercise but only visualized doing the workout done by Group Two, experienced a 24-percent gain in strength—close to the result produced by Group Two. How could that happen without them even having to sweat? The answer is that the placebo effect is so powerful it changes the way both our brain and body work, and because of this it can provide a nearly equivalent strength-building benefit as actually working out. I know it sounds wacky, but it's hard to argue with results.

Another study, done by Harvard psychologist Ellen Langer and published in *Psychological Science* in February 2007, clearly demonstrated how the placebo effect is attributed to a person's beliefs and expectations. In this study, one group of housekeeping staff in a major hotel was told that what they did on a daily basis qualified as the amount of exercise needed to be fit and healthy. They were told how many calories they burned while doing different housekeeping activities, and this information was put up on a poster in the housekeepers' lounges to serve as a reminder. They didn't make any changes in behavior, they just kept doing their job the same way they always did and, surprisingly, four weeks later, those housekeepers had lost weight, had lower blood pressure, and had an improved BMI (body mass index). A similar group of housekeepers was a control group that had not been told that their job qualified as exercise. The control group saw none of the improvements experienced by the test group. The study showed that what a person believes to be true will alter their physiological response to it. Just by changing their beliefs that their jobs were exercise had a positive impact on their health and weight.

The Importance of Believing in the Right Things

Retirement success is directly impacted by a retiree's own attitude about aging that has built up over the years. The problem is, because of all the negative stereotyping of older people being

LESSONS FROM A PANDEMIC

People with a negative attitude had a hard time coping with all the changes they were experiencing during the COVID-19 crisis and ended up getting angry and frustrated. They believed there was nothing they could do to improve their situation, which was a big mistake. Sitting on the couch cracking open another bottle of wine while watching more news about the virus and how the world seemed to be falling apart only increased their negativity.

How you thought about things in those trying times of self-isolation, job loss, and uncertainty had a direct impact on how you felt, and people who looked at everything negatively didn't feel very good at all. Getting through the pandemic in one piece was all about gratitude. It was about appreciating what we had, and sometimes what we didn't have.

Watching the news and how the health care workers and first responders stood up for us gave some much-needed perspective about how many good people there are out there in the world. The crisis opened our eyes to the important roles played by the grocery clerks, the shelf-stockers, the carriers who deliver food and other necessities, the bus drivers providing public transit, and the people volunteering at food banks—and the risks they were all taking. It made our own problems seem pretty insignificant compared to what they were going through. It was a time to be thankful for the help of others.

The pandemic opened our eyes to how lucky many of us are. We had enough food, a roof over our heads, our family and friends, and above all, our health. There was a lot to be grateful for.

frail, forgetful, having low energy, and so on, most retirees have a negative view about aging; and based on the placebo effect, we know that what we believe about aging affects how we age. In other words, if you have a negative attitude about aging and believe it will be awful, you are screwed before you even start. You need to appreciate how strong your mind really is and how your beliefs about retirement will determine your retirement outcome. Retirement Heaven or Hell? It's all in your head (or at least it is to a great degree).

> The thing always happens that you really believe in; and the belief in a thing makes it happen.
>
> —Frank Lloyd Wright

What current beliefs or attitudes are holding you back? Following are some examples of negative beliefs about retirement that could be limiting your ability to thrive at this stage of your life:

- I need to stay in my comfort zone and play it safe, so I don't get hurt.
- I'm too old to learn that.
- I'm not good enough to find a job at this stage in my life.
- I'm not smart enough to start my own business.
- I can't lose weight.
- I'm not a good writer.
- I could never get up on stage and give a speech.
- I'm not good at socializing.
- I'm scared to join a tribe.
- Physical and cognitive decline are inevitable and there's nothing I can do to stop them or slow them down.

Get out your journal and make a list of the limiting views that are holding you back from enjoying a great retirement. Once you are finished, rip that page of excuses out of your journal and tear it up into small pieces and throw it into the garbage because none of it is true. You need to get rid of these negative beliefs because all the stuff you wrote about yourself is bullshit. You need to stop allowing these old beliefs/excuses/lies (call them whatever you want) to prevent you from enjoying an awesome Victory Lap.

Retirement success is all about having the right attitude and the belief that what you are doing works. If you believe that you can lose the weight, get the job, or have an awesome retirement, and then you put in the time and effort, guess what—you will succeed. So, my question to you is: When you know what you need to do, why wouldn't you do it? The answer in most cases is fear.

Getting Over Your Fears

Your mind is where your fear lives and it's where the mother of all battles will take place, the one between your insecurities and your newly found retirement beliefs and objectives. If you lack confidence to take the leap into retirement—to start a new, exciting phase of your life in Victory Lap and attempt the things you've been dreaming of and yearning to do—you are not alone.

> Fear and self-doubt have always been the greatest enemies of human potential.
>
> —Brian Tracy

Everyone suffers from the same kinds of retirement fears, but most people are scared, embarrassed or ashamed to admit their own, and so they end up suffering in silence. It's important to understand that you are not alone. What you are experiencing is basic human nature; you're not thinking any different from anyone else. Trust me, I've talked to thousands of retirees and everyone feels the same inside. We are scared to apply for a job because people will think we are too old, and that fear of being rejected keeps us from potentially getting a job we might enjoy and that would keep us engaged and challenged. We are scared to start a new business because we fear that we are not good enough and it might fail. Do me a favor and get over it. You need to stop hiding and watching your retirement dreams slowly evaporate just because you're afraid.

Fear, that inner gremlin that lives in your head, is known by many names. Seth Godin refers to it as "the lizard brain"; Steven Pressfield, author of the best-seller *The War of Art*, calls it "the resistance"; and Steven Chapman, a writer specializing in nurturing creativity, calls it "the inner critic." Call it what you want, but at the end of the day, it's the same thing: a force that can stop you in your tracks and make you afraid to even start.

Your inner gremlin has good intentions, oddly enough, and tries to protect you by making all change seem like a threat. It wants you to stay safe by not taking any risks. It knows where you are most vulnerable, and that is where it will attack, focusing on what you think you can't do or be. You need to be prepared for when your inner gremlin comes roaring out of the little hole it lives in, yelling that you're not good enough, that you're not smart enough, that you're going to fail and end up getting hurt. It will try to beat you up and make you feel like a loser, hoping to scare you back into playing safe. What your inner gremlin fails to see, though, is that without change, you have no hope and nothing to look forward to in retirement.

The best way to deal with fear is to face it, because when you do, it stops growing. Now is the time to corner that gremlin, stare him in the eye for the first time and finally say, "I'm tired of always giving in to you. I'm not going to live your way anymore." But be careful, because when he hears what you are

> If it scares you, it might be a good thing to try
>
> —Seth Godin

planning to do, it will really shake him up and all hell will break loose. Think of it as the equivalent of grabbing a large alligator by the tail. But if you have faith and are committed to hanging on, you will soon discover that he is not so powerful after all. He is a fraud, but he has been able to get away with it all these years because you have been afraid to confront him. What a waste, allowing him to control you for so many years and keep you from attempting great things.

Instead of trying something new and taking any chances, most of us take the easy path and stick with what we know because we have been conditioned to play it safe. But it's important to understand that along with that comfort comes a lack of true happiness from never trying. It is such a waste of life being afraid to travel outside of your comfort zone because you are afraid of change and uncertainty, of possibly failing and showing people that you "were not good enough."

> The cost of being wrong is less than the cost of doing nothing.
> —Seth Godin

It's a mistake to let your fear push you into avoiding certain things. Don't let it limit you and turn you into a retirement victim. Don't avoid things you perceive as too challenging. Don't avoid learning new complex things. Don't default to the ordinary and hide behind the standard excuses (I'm too old, I'm not smart enough, and others).

Fear is the primary roadblock that keeps retirees from learning and growing. But at the end of the day, none of us is getting out of here alive; we are all going to die. It's silly at this point in our lives to give in to fear of failure or possible embarrassment, because it really doesn't matter anymore. So, don't let fear limit you in retirement and prevent you from realizing your full potential. This is the time to take back control of your life; the time to take some risks and

> If you want to conquer fear, don't sit home and think about it. Go out and get busy.
> —Dale Carnegie

see what happens. It's time to do the uncomfortable and painful things, because those are the things that make retirement interesting and worth living. If not now, when?

I Think I Can! I Think I Can!

If you can't push through your fear, you will never experience triumph. The power of positive thinking can take you there. Remember the difference your attitude can make? It can literally change the way your life turns out, for the better. And, as Theodore Roosevelt said, the act of trying is an achievement in itself:

> *It is not the critic who counts; not the man who points out how the strong man stumbles, or where the doer of deeds could have done them better. The credit belongs to the man who is actually in the arena, whose face is marred by dust and sweat and blood; who strives valiantly; who errs, who comes short again and again, because there is no effort without error and shortcoming; but who does actually strive to do the deeds; who knows great enthusiasms, the great devotions; who spends himself in a worthy cause; who at the best knows in the end the triumph of high achievement, and who at the worst, if he fails, at least fails while daring greatly, so that his place shall never be with those cold and timid souls who neither know victory nor defeat.*
>
> *—Theodore Roosevelt*

You always have a choice when it comes to how you see the world. Instead of problems, see challenges; instead of being scared by a retirement goal, feel the thrill of excitement; instead of worrying endlessly, take action. Whether your retirement outcome is positive or negative is entirely up to you, and it depends to a large degree on the attitude you bring to it. So, choose to be happy, healthy, and fulfilled!

Of course, you can't avoid having some fears about retirement—it's a huge change in your life and so many things are unknown. The point is to harness those fears: acknowledge them, face them, and use them to motivate you to take appropriate action so you can achieve the retirement outcomes you are after. Giving in to your fears is a sure path to Retirement Hell. But overcoming them will help you create your own little piece of heaven in your Victory Lap.

> Sometimes all you need is twenty seconds of insane courage. Just, literally, twenty seconds of embarrassing bravery. And I promise you, something great will come of it.
>
> —Matt Damon
> in the movie
> *We Bought a Zoo*

Choosing to be positive can take you a long way to a heavenly retirement, and taking action will take you even further. For example, a lot of people lose a lot of sleep worrying that they haven't saved enough for retirement, but much of the time that's their own fault, really, because they don't have a good handle on how much money they really need. They simply avoid the whole question because they're afraid of it. But if they just face it and take the necessary actions to ensure their financial independence, it will eliminate the fear of the unknown and set them up for a worry-free, heavenly retirement.

Dying Without Trying Is One of Life's Greatest Tragedies

If you don't feel some kind of fear about retirement and you don't have any butterflies because of the things you want to do and try, it's probably because you're not stretching outside your comfort zone enough and what you have planned for retirement doesn't look a whole lot different than your life now. If, however, your mind is racing with both excitement and a bit of anxiety, that's a good sign that you're doing what you need to do. Struggling a little and feeling uncomfortable are prerequisites for achieving Retirement Heaven. The biggest failure you can

> It's only after you've stepped outside your comfort zone that you begin to change, grow, and transform.
>
> —Roy T. Bennett

encounter would be not trying to create your dream retirement and then being haunted by regret, knowing that you had a shot but were too afraid to take it.

Remember, You Have Been Through This Before

One of the benefits of being at this stage in life is your experience. Use it to your advantage, to help cultivate that all-important positive attitude. Think back to every major thing you've accomplished in life—those times when you were "all in," like asking that cute girl to dance who eventually became your wife, or trying for that big promotion at work and getting it. Sure, at the time you felt some combination of fear, doubt, anticipation, and trepidation. But because you tried and succeeded, those are some of the things you're most proud of; the things that brought you the most meaning and happiness. The same feeling will return to you in retirement if you decide to challenge yourself and reach for something great.

You always have a choice. You can let your fear keep you from finding another job, starting a new business, traveling to a foreign land, joining a gym, finding a tribe, or meeting new friends. Or you can decide to generate twenty seconds of courage and change your life forever. Why settle for a mediocre retirement when you are capable and deserving of so much more?

My Story

I never used to be afraid until I went to work full-time. My way of combatting my fear was to try to fit in by working harder than anyone else, and that worked for a while, until I got married and had kids. Starting a family changed everything, and that's when the fear started to creep back in. I became scared that people didn't like me, that maybe I wasn't good enough, that I might get fired, and that, if I did, I could never get another job that paid as well. The fear at times was all-consuming and resulted in a lot of sleepless nights.

My fear caused me to work even harder to outperform and be what I thought was safe. But it cost me time and enjoyment with my family, and I also started to fear that perhaps I was losing their love because I was working so much. My fears seemed to pile up around this point in my life, but things changed for the better when the company decided to show me the door.

Today in Victory Lap I no longer live in fear and everything that I do is aligned with my values. I'm focusing on spending quality time with my family and friends because I know that, at the end of the day, those are the things that really matter. I have also gone on to try and succeed at some amazing things like speaking in front of an audience and starting my own business, and I don't plan on stopping there. I'm not afraid anymore because, at my age, I figure I really don't have anything to lose by trying, so why not?

My belief is that if I follow the nine retirement principles and do the right things, I will enjoy a long, healthy Victory Lap. It's as simple as that. I expect the next ten years to be the best of my life because I have a lot of fun and I've listed lots of challenging things on my dance card—things that I couldn't do when I was working full-time. I also feel better about how things turned out for me. Before, I held a lot of resentment over my old job and how they treated me; but today that feeling has changed to one of gratitude as I can see all the benefits I derived from my career. Working at the bank provided security for my family and allowed me to learn a lot about coaching people and how to run a successful business, which are things I use today in my Victory Lap.

Gratitude is a new strength of mine, and I use it to appreciate what I have. I wake up and go to bed every day feeling grateful. I have a loving family and good friends. I have a nice roof over my head, and the kids are doing great. I have my health and have created a great job for myself that gives me purpose and money so I can do a lot of different things. Retirement is good when you look at it the right way.

Questions for Self-Reflection

- Do you have a positive mental outlook?
- Are you able to accept change?
- Are you confident? Do you believe in what you are trying to do?
- Is your current attitude an asset or liability?
- What are your retirement beliefs?
- What is your inner critic saying? Do you believe him/her?
- Is your self-talk positive or negative?
- What are you afraid of?
- What would you do if you weren't afraid?
- When was the last time you took a real risk? Do you remember how that actually feels?
- What's the worst thing that would happen if what you are attempting doesn't work out? What would happen if it did work out?

Rating Retirement Principle #8

How would you rate the following on a scale of 1–10:

- your attitude?
- the power of your beliefs?
- your sense of gratitude?

What things can you start doing today to get each of these ratings to a 10?

Simple Truths

- Enjoying a great retirement is an attitude.
- In retirement, what you believe in is what you will get. If you believe your retirement will suck—guess what? It will.
- If you think old, you become old.
- Most retirees who fail in retirement do so because of their limiting beliefs about what's possible for them and what they are capable of achieving in retirement.
- It's a big mistake to let your fear and insecurities determine your fate. Fear has killed more dreams than failure ever did.
- The possible only becomes possible when you believe it is.
- If you believe you can—you will.
- Having a good attitude coupled with optimism, hope, and faith will ground you during uncertain times and improve your health and longevity.
- To change your retirement outcome, you need to change your beliefs and the way you think.

12

Retirement Principle #9

Discover Your Purpose

Success is waking up in the morning, whoever you are, wherever you are, however old you are, and bounding out of bed because there's something out there that you love to do, that you believe in, that you're good at, something that's bigger than you are. And you can hardly wait to get at it again today.
—*Whit Hobbs*

A successful retirement requires much more than just having a lot of money. Money may allow you to sleep better at night, but in addition to money you also need a purpose-driven life of meaningful activities that will allow you to wake up each morning excited to get out of bed. We are all genetically programmed to need purpose, our own "why"—a sense of inspiration and vitality in our lives. To ignore this fact will result in boredom and lack of direction. Besides, you didn't come this far just to endure your remaining life and kill time, did you? You need to create a life for yourself that has meaning, passion, and purpose at its core.

If you are a growth-oriented retiree, you will need to find a way of filling the big hole that was left behind after leaving your full-time job. It should be something that replaces the positive aspects of a career; something that is challenging and requires you to learn new things; something that allows you to contribute and feel that you are a valuable contributor; something that involves social interaction; something that you can get lost in and makes the time fly by.

LESSONS FROM A PANDEMIC

Many of us felt a loss of purpose during the COVID-19 pandemic. If you couldn't work from home, there wasn't much in the way of meaningful things to do, outside of trying to survive. Not having a sense of purpose made us feel a little lost and disoriented. We started to feel frustrated and antsy because we didn't know what to do with all the free time on our hands.

Some of us began to realize that our job was way better than just puttering around the house and taking the dog out for another walk around the block. In retirement, you can live like this for a while and even enjoy the downtime, but living too long without purpose quickly becomes Retirement Hell.

Meaningful Contribution: Purpose

Finding purpose is a unique journey for each of us. Purpose comes in many different shapes and sizes, and most people have more than one. In retirement, purpose isn't just about golfing and exotic travel. It's also about serving a cause larger than yourself and about leaving the world in better shape than you found it. Your purpose could be based on eldercare, taking care of the grandkids, taking care of your garden or pets, volunteering at the hospital, or simply cutting lawns for others who are not able.

If work remains part of your *raison d'être*—be it for the challenge, the social aspect, the structure if gives your life, or maybe the money if provides to help support your retirement lifestyle—you don't have to commit to a career at this stage, and you don't have to dedicate an enormous amount of your time to work. It's OK to do a job just to generate a little extra "fun money." The key is to do whatever makes you feel good about yourself; whatever makes you feel that you still contribute and that you still matter. A successful Victory Lap doesn't have to be more complicated than that. But, then again, some of you might decide to swing for the fences and start your own business or write a couple of books, like I did. That's all right too. Whatever floats your boat, as they say. We'll explore finding meaningful work in your Victory Lap in much more detail in Chapter 15.

> A passionate interest in what you do is the secret of enjoying life, perhaps the secret of a long life, whether it is helping old people or children, or making cheese, or growing earthworms.
>
> —Julia Child

The Rewards of Aging with Purpose

Okinawans, residents of a small chain of Japanese islands, are some of the longest-living people on the planet. They don't stress about retirement because it's hard to worry about something when you don't even have a word in your language for it. Instead, they are concerned throughout their lives with finding and maintaining *ikigai*, which roughly translated means "a reason to live."

Everyone needs an *ikigai*, and if you don't have one it's time to start worrying, because without an enduring feeling of purpose, you will not live as long as others. It's been shown that people who have a sense of purpose or direction in life outlive their peers.

A 2008 study in Japan found that people who experienced *ikigai* lived longer than people who did not have a sense of purpose.

In fact, numerous studies have linked having a purpose to improved well-being, including better sleep; fewer strokes and heart attacks; and a lower risk of dementia, disability, and premature death. In one study of six thousand people over a fourteen-year period, it was found that people with a sense of purpose were 15-percent less likely to die than those who said they were more or less aimless. Another study analyzed how purpose influences a person's risk of dementia, finding that people who had a greater sense of purpose were 2.4 times less likely to develop Alzheimer's.

> Having a purpose and knowing exactly what your values are will add additional years to your life.
>
> —Dan Buettner

Finding Your Purpose Is a Process

Some people are born with a mission and never lose sight of it throughout their life, but that is not as common as you might think. More frequently, we sublimate our true purpose during our working years, replacing our mission with that of the Corp's, or we sacrifice our personal mission to fulfill the needs of our family. Now that those obligations are all behind you, or are soon to be, how will you rediscover your purpose in life, your *ikigai*? Chances are, it won't reveal itself to you fully formed; you'll have to go searching for it.

The next part of this book, Part 3, is all about taking that journey. First you need to go inside and reconnect with who you really are—your values and intrinsic needs—to figure out what you want and need to be happy and fulfilled. In Chapter 13 we will go through the exploration and reconnecting part, and in Chapter 14 we will help you discover the values that drive you and make you happy.

For many successful growth-oriented retirees, purpose equals meaningful work. Whenever I read a story about someone who's managed to live to a hundred or beyond, I always look for common traits that might explain how they did it. I have found that one of the most common things is that they still work or volunteer in some way late in life. Because they love the work that they do, whatever it is they choose to do and to whatever extent, it serves as a deep source of nourishment for their spirit and they end up living longer than most. (In Chapter 15, we'll explore in detail how you might choose to work in retirement, and to what extent.) The important thing to understand is that these people don't work because they have to make more money; they do it because it gives them a sense of purpose and it makes them feel good because it delivers on some of their values and retirement goals. Purpose is something that we need until our last breath, and even having a lot of money will never change that.

My Story

For many years, working and taking care of my family gave me all the purpose and meaning I needed. But when my kids were able to stand on their own two feet and the mortgage was paid off, I lost that sense of purpose and needed to find a suitable replacement. I know myself well enough to realize that if I don't have a meaningful, purpose-driven life, I'm going to be in trouble. The thought of spending twenty-plus years doing nothing—being bored and feeling useless—makes me shudder. I'm wired to work. I have an innate need to contribute, to achieve, and to be part of something. Without some kind of work, I wouldn't be able to satisfy some of my core values, and because of that it would be hard for me to be happy in retirement.

I owe my strong sense of purpose to my parents, because it's they who taught me firsthand how important purpose is to a happy life. Following are two real-life lessons I learned from them about finding new purpose in retirement.

A Story About My Father

My father was both frugal and money smart, and even though he immigrated to this country with little in the way of money, between him and my mother they were able to build an adequate "nest egg" to support a comfortable retirement. My mother retired before my father, and her main purpose was taking care of her family and socializing with her friends. She got into a pattern of watching *The Price Is Right* at ten in the morning and then going out for coffee or lunch with her friends, returning home to watch a few soap operas in the afternoon. When my father retired, he tried to follow the same pattern, but it wasn't long before he cracked, suffering from a bad case of retirement shock that lasted for the better part of a year.

Dad would constantly tell us the same old stories from his working days, and it was clear he missed the purpose and direction he was so used to having when he had a career. His reminiscing started getting to my mother and me. One morning at the breakfast table when he started up again, she tossed the classifieds from the newspaper at him with a few part-time jobs circled and said, "Here! Stop whining and go find a part-time job for yourself." (My mom was Irish, can you tell?) So, my father went out that morning and, before the day was over, he had found himself a part-time job.

When I found out what that job was, I couldn't stop laughing. You see, he used to run an accounting department for a large company, where he managed a group of about sixty people, and now he had gotten a part-time job delivering pet food for a small retail pet food store. His job was to drive a van two days a week and deliver pet food to people who couldn't make it into the store, mostly the elderly.

Once he had that job, my father was a changed man—it gave him the purpose that he was missing, and he loved it. The job was only part-time, and he had a simple role compared to his previous career, but he enjoyed getting out and feeling useful, and helping the elderly made him feel especially good. It just goes to show that purpose doesn't need to be much to be powerful. Having a reason to get up and out at least a couple days a week cured my father from the retirement shock he was suffering from, and even better, he didn't have to watch those soap operas anymore!

Soon enough, my dad was able to contribute to the business in an even more meaningful way. The owner of the store was struggling a little, as he was new and inexperienced with running a business; my father, with all his business experience, was able to step in and serve as his mentor. Helping the store owner and feeling needed by someone made my father feel even better.

The important lesson here is that because my father was a growth-oriented retiree who identified closely with his past career, sitting around watching TV with my mother couldn't fill that big hole that was created when he left his work life behind. He needed more, and that simple job delivered it to him in spades. But there's more.

When my father was able to use his gifts and skills to help others who were struggling, he experienced something referred to as a "helper's high." It's similar to the "high" that runners experience during a long run. The exercise causes the release of the feel-good chemicals oxytocin, serotonin, and dopamine, which results in a feeling of pure elation. Helping others impacted my father in a similar fashion. Whenever he made deliveries to people in need or helped the owner solve a business problem, he experienced another "happiness hit." Helping others boosted his mood because he knew he still mattered, and knowing this made him feel happy inside. You could say he was high on helping, because doing good makes you feel good—a natural high if there ever was one.

A Story About My Mother

My mother was a comfort-oriented retiree and her main role was taking care of her family. She loved doing it and found her worth through her relationship with others. She was dedicated to her family, raising her children, and later she served as a caregiver for my father when he became ill.

My father passed away at age seventy-two from pancreatic cancer, and after that, my mother had no one left at home to give her energy to; no one to share herself with. When you lose your role as a mother and provider, you lose a lot. Mothers need to feel needed; they need to feel useful. And when they do, they will live longer and better than most.

The day after Dad's passing, a cat appeared at my mother's back door and wouldn't leave. Unable to find its owner, Mum took that cat in and gave it a home. Boots, so named because of his four white feet, put meaning back into my mother's life and they became inseparable. That cat made her happy and gave her a new purpose: Boots needed her, and she needed Boots. She always thought that my father had sent Boots to her to keep her company and give her a reason for living after he had to leave, and I think she's right.

Questions for Self-Reflection
- Can you list three purposeful undertakings that you plan on doing during your Victory Lap?
- What do you think you would be good at?
- What would you enjoy doing?
- Do you know what drives you, what activity gets your juices flowing?
- What activities do you find completely absorbing? What things can you get lost in?
- Do you feel like you are living with a sense of purpose? Why or why not?

Rating Retirement Principle #9
How would you rate your sense of having a purpose on a scale of 1–10? What do you need to do to get the rating to a 10?

Simple Truths
- The most fulfilled retirements are the most purposeful retirements.
- Having a good reason to get out of bed in the morning will add years to your retirement and improve the quality of those years.
- If you don't have purpose, you will shorten your lifespan and get older faster.
- Every retiree needs a sense of mission, a "why" to live for.
- In Victory Lap there is a reawakening of purpose and time to finally fulfill that purpose.
- A sense of fulfillment and achievement is essential for a successful Victory Lap.
- There is no better purpose than making sure the ones we love and care about are doing well.

Part 2 Summary

The Nine Retirement Principles

The nine principles are the basic building blocks of retirement lifestyle design. They are the necessary ingredients that make retirement exciting and worth living. Without having them all in place, your retirement will be out of balance. Doing well in only one or two areas at the cost of others never works.

Before, when you were working full-time you could blame your job for why you couldn't be the parent, spouse, or friend you wanted to be. Because of the demands of your job, you didn't have the time to exercise or eat properly. But this excuse is gone once you retire, and you now have time to fix things by making the principles the focus of your retirement.

If you are unsure about what to work on first, that's OK. Figuring out what not to do is just as important as figuring out what to do. Start by getting rid of the things you don't want. Maybe you don't want to be overweight anymore. Maybe you don't want high blood pressure anymore. Maybe you don't want to be lonely anymore. Maybe you don't want to have a poor relationship with your kids anymore. Make a list in your journal of the things you don't want, and start working on those things so you can get them out of the way before working on the good stuff.

Using the principles to reduce the number of decisions you need to make on a daily basis will mean less stress and a simpler life. Eventually, without requiring you to think, these nine principles will automatically dictate what you eat, how much you drink, how much you exercise, how much time you spend watching TV, and how you spend your free time. An added bonus is that they will keep you away from possible temptation. They will be the compass on your retirement journey, helping to keep you on the path you create for yourself.

But you need to be careful, because satisfying a principle is a mistake if it comes at the cost of another one. If, for example, you decide to find new purpose through starting a business and you work so hard that it negatively affects your health or it takes too much time away from investing in your relationships, you need to rethink things. Also, you do not want to make too many changes in a short period of time, which will end up driving you a little crazy. The principles are meant to reduce stress, not create more. Start slow, stay in balance, and things will improve over time.

Following the principles will put you in the best state possible for accomplishing what you want in retirement. They will help you achieve your dreams and give you that sense of fulfillment you are looking for. But while the nine principles will provide you with a strong foundation, they alone will not guarantee the heavenly retirement you are hoping for. Creating your own personal plan for your Victory Lap is essential; one that is based on your personal values and goals. And that's what the rest of this book is all about.

Questions for Self-Reflection
- Do you believe in the power of the nine retirement principles?
- Are you willing to make them a part of your daily life?
- What did you learn about yourself after rating the principles?
- What areas are you satisfied with?
- What areas are you concerned about and feel need immediate work?

Simple Truths
- Many retirees are clueless about how to spend their next twenty-plus years in a meaningful way.
- It's hard to focus on finding purpose when you are worried about money.
- If you want your life to be different, you'll need to think and act differently.
- If you make following the nine retirement principles a habit, you are more likely to enjoy an awesome retirement.
- By following the nine retirement principles, you can make smart lifestyle choices, find new purpose, and slow down the rate of aging.
- The most successful retirees have a clear vision and follow the nine retirement principles to make that vision a reality.

PART 3

SEARCHING FOR YOUR PURPOSE

13

Self-Knowledge

The Key to Retirement Success

Can you remember who you were before the world told you who you should be?
—Charles Bukowski

When we were young, many of us had a sense of what our reason for being was, but that feeling faded as time went on and we allowed ourselves to be turned into something that was not us. The passion and enthusiasm of youth often dissipate when the demands of work and family priorities take over. Soon, we are following what someone else wants for us or what we think others expect of us. No wonder so many people feel lost when they finally stop working and have the time to take stock.

Realizing you've lost your identity and your passion in life can send you straight to Retirement Hell, or this can be a second chance at being who you truly are and focusing on what really drives you. The choice is yours and the route you take depends on your attitude. Choosing to think of retirement as your Victory Lap is a second chance for you to find real joy, perhaps more than you ever had in your working life. This is your opportunity to feel like a kid again (remember, this is a beginning, not an ending)—to rediscover your passion and do what excites you.

At some point as we near the end of the honeymoon stage of retirement or start the journey out of Retirement Hell, something inside us (our innate needs) begins to push us to follow our mission and do what we were brought into this world to do. Not all of us will experience this, but most growth-oriented retirees will. Call it unfinished business, and we won't be happy until we satisfy that feeling within us. The feeling of needing to live an authentic life and refusing to pretend anymore; of no longer being satisfied to just fit in and survive. When we reach a point where we are past that, we will be unwilling to live like that anymore. But before we can figure out what we should do with our lives, what our purpose is, we need to reconnect with who we really are and get a good handle on what our values are.

LESSONS FROM A PANDEMIC

The COVID-19 pandemic was a life-changing event in so many ways. The virus changed our collective perspective, and we now view life and the world around us with a different set of eyes. The isolation gave us lots of time to take stock and ponder things. Our inner voice started talking to us about the changes we needed to make in our lives once we got our freedom back.

What did you learn from the pandemic? Are you happy with the way your life is going? What changes do you intend to make? Who do you need to become? What do you need to do?

Reconnect with Who You Are

We are all in the process of creating a movie about our lives, a movie in which we are the star, and one that is only partly finished. In this chapter we will help you to use your movie to get reacquainted with yourself—your strengths, your struggles, and the traits of the character that is the old you.

Watching the movie of your own life will take you back on your journey since childhood. This will remind you about what made you happy, which in turn will help you to discover your purpose(s) and passions and, ultimately, the person you were meant to be. You really want to go deep inside yourself and think about why things turned out the way they did and how you can improve things going forward.

> If you want to understand today, you have to search yesterday.
> —Pearl S. Buck

You can learn a lot about yourself by watching your personal movie; the process allows you to step back and see the cause–effect relationships between the choices you made and how your life has unfolded as a consequence; how you got to where you are now. Take your time watching your movie and learn from it. Look for patterns both good and bad. Look for the different ways you limited yourself. Look for sources of flow; things that made you become lost in what you were doing, when time just flew by because you were so focused. Look for the things that make you happy and what didn't.

Watching your movie can be uncomfortable at times, because when you dig deep and take a really good look at your life, you aren't going to like everything you see. You will see how you messed up, probably more

> Oh yes, the past can hurt. But the way I see it, you can either run from it or learn from it.
> —Rafiki quote from *The Lion King*

than a few times, and you'll realize that many times this could have been avoided if you had allowed someone to guide and mentor you. Guys are especially bad at this because we hate asking for help—we don't want to admit to anyone that we don't know and could sure use their help.

Sometimes we feel shame about not having been authentic, usually at work, and that shame has stuck with us until now, when we bring it to the surface by watching our movie. Just remember that nobody's movie is perfect. Everyone's movie has both good and bad stuff; good days and bad days. We all make mistakes and compromises while struggling to get through life. Be kind to yourself and recognize the good and the bad for what they are. The point is to learn from this process of self-discovery and to use your observations to make the changes you want in your life going forward.

Watching your movie will force you to face the things you have been avoiding so that you can take corrective action before it is too late. And it will help you to recognize the things in life that truly move you. Those are the things to focus on and strive for to create a retirement lifestyle that you find heavenly. Your movie will help you understand your motivation for doing some of the things that you did, and your true mission in life, which you will feel emerging as you relive your past and look for patterns. You will learn a lot about yourself as you watch your progression from child, to student, to worker, to retirement. And the self-knowledge that you gain in this process is foundational to creating the plan for your Victory Lap—to rediscovering joy and fulfillment at this stage of your life.

So, get some popcorn and find a comfy chair. It's time to watch your movie and get a good understanding of why your life turned out the way it did, what made you the person you are today, and to discover the life you want to live from this point forward.

Become a Child Again

When we are young, our self-esteem is at an all-time high. We have confidence in our abilities and feel that there is nothing that we can't do. At this stage we have a strong sense of self and the world is our oyster, but this frequently changes as we get older and the fear and expectations of others set in. We all have childhood dreams about who we want to be and what we want to do when we grow up, but unfortunately for many of us those dreams never come true. How sad is that?

Think back to your childhood. What did you want to be when you grew up? I remember that I wanted to be a police officer or a firefighter. They are heroes; they help people who are in trouble, and they're respected and looked up to for what they do. That childhood dream makes sense to me today when I think about it, because I have always had this strong need to help and protect people. That is important to me. I want to be liked and respected. But neither of those occupations worked out for me, because my parents considered them dangerous and convinced me to do something else. Parents fear for us and urge us to make choices driven by practical considerations, which many times are in conflict with what we really want. I still wonder, how would my life be different today had I decided not to listen and had become a firefighter?

Do you remember your parents ever saying, "How could you possibly support your wife/husband/partner/kids/lifestyle with that job?" I sure do. Now is the time to revisit those early dreams and motivations to understand what your mission is in life and how you can plan to make your Victory Lap meaningful by fulfilling it.

Questions for Self-Reflection
- What are some of your favorite childhood memories?
- What kinds of things did you like to do as a child?
- Who were your heroes?

- What were you good at?
- What hobbies did you have?
- What sports did you play?
- Did you like team sports or individual sports?
- What talents of yours did you not have a chance to develop fully?
- What awards did you win?
- What did you dream about being?
- What did you abandon that you'd like to reclaim?

The School Years

In school we were taught to compete and strive to be better than everyone else. Remember how we used to compare marks to see who were the smartest kids? We were socialized to believe that the better we stack up against others, the more people will respect and like us because everyone loves a winner. Teachers punished us for non-compliance and rewarded us for obedience. In this way, schools are pretty good at teaching compliance, and Corps love that fact about them because they want productive workers who will toe the line and fit well within their system. No wonder so many workers dislike their jobs today!

For many, our school experience is the first time our self-esteem is put to the test. We are afraid of not getting good marks or not getting into a good school. We start comparing ourselves with others in terms of who has the most friends, who has the better grades, or who scored the most goals. What were you afraid of in school? How do you think that influenced how your life turned out?

Questions for Self-Reflection
- What subjects did you like in school?
- Which teachers did you like? Why?
- What didn't you like about school?
- Which crowd did you hang out with? What was your role?
- If you could go back and do school all over again, what would you do differently?

The Working Years

Just like in school, in the Corp we are taught to seek superiority over others in order to achieve success. We chase after recognition, wealth, and status, while constantly comparing ourselves to people who are more "successful." We adopt the mentality that they are better than us because they have a bigger title and a bigger office and they make more money. We then spend our careers working to correct the imbalance, much to our employer's delight. And to compete, we allow ourselves to become just like the other corporate soldiers. We learn to dress like them, act like them, and talk like them.

The Corp always wants us to keep hungry, to keep competing with our peers. Hungry to earn more and spend more so we can show off our success. The Corp celebrates "winners" who don't know how to stop, who are willing to sacrifice their relationships with their families and friends. These are the people who win all the prizes and trinkets because they are willing to sacrifice more than anyone else. But are they really winners?

In order to survive and become successful, we force ourselves to be what our employers want us to be. We follow their mission, not our own. Over time we lose our sense of self, our self-esteem, our deeply held beliefs about what is right—all in the pursuit of security for our families. But really, what else could you do at the time? Similar to what we experienced in school, the Corp demanded we give up who we were, become compliant and obedient, and accept its version of the dream. But being willing to do that came at the cost of us not being who we really are.

Questions for Self-Reflection
- Was your career a good fit?
- Were you authentic at work?
- What changes did you have to make to work there?
- What did you like about your work?

- What didn't you like about your work?
- What didn't you know you would be good at?
- What comes naturally/easily to you?
- What skills and traits do others most admire in you?
- What accomplishments made you feel most proud? This is an important question, as it points to the real you. By answering it, you will see what is really important to you.

Accept the Movie of Your Life for What It Is

At some point while watching your movie, you may have a realization that you have been living the life everyone told you to live instead of the one you wanted, the one you know deep inside you should have lived. You see all the mistakes made and the fears and bad habits that held you back, and you begin to ask yourself questions. Why didn't I look after my health better? Why didn't I stay close to my friends? Why didn't I spend more quality time with my family? Why did I stay so long in a job that I didn't like anymore? Why did I waste so much money buying useless things? Why didn't I save more for retirement? You see how you were socialized toward prioritizing making a lot of money and buying a lot of stuff so that you could prove you are better than everyone else. You come to realize that living like that came at a high cost, the cost of your well-being, and this makes you mad because you have been played, and you know it.

Learning from the past is key for future retirement success. While you can't go back and edit the past, the good news is that you can learn from it and make the necessary adjustments required to change the trajectory of your future. Use your movie to make peace with your past and eliminate any possible regret.

> You can't go back and change the beginning, but you can start where you are and change the ending.
>
> —C.S. Lewis

Everyone makes mistakes; nobody's perfect. What you need to do is accept ownership of where you went wrong, recognize how and why you lost your passion and spark, and learn from your past so you can avoid making the same mistakes again. Also, take from your movie the happy experiences and the goals, dreams, and values that still resonate with you. Taking stock of what made you happy before and still does now and incorporating those things into your plan for your Victory Lap will help you create a heavenly retirement.

Review the past to understand how you got to where you are and to help you figure out what you need to change so you can achieve the happy ending you want. But don't get stuck in the past, regretting golden days you feel you'll never get back. You will impact your retirement future by focusing on the present, because it is the only thing you can control. Learn from your movie, start doing the right things daily, and the future will take care of itself.

My Movie; My Story

> *I can't think of a sadder way to die than with the knowledge that I never showed up in this world as who I really am. I can't think of a more graced way to die than with the knowledge that I showed up here as my true self, the best I knew how, able to engage life freely and lovingly because I had become fierce with reality.*
>
> —*Parker J. Palmer*

Watching my movie was a big wake-up call for me and gave me an opportunity to come to terms with my past. I could clearly see how both my sense of self and my self-esteem eroded over time as I went from being a young boy, then going to school, and finally ending up in the Corp.

I didn't do very well in high school academically, as I was consumed by sports and just wasn't into some of the teachers or some of the courses they forced us to take, like calculus. Because of my mediocre marks I couldn't get into everyone's definition of a "good university" and ended up at Ryerson Polytechnical Institute in Toronto (as it was known then), where I excelled. I remember telling myself that it was time to get serious and focus on getting good grades so I could get a good job. I loved that school and it was a good fit for me. (Although Ryerson at that time wasn't a university, so I never did get a degree, and this would come back and cost me later in my working career.)

When I finished school, I had no idea about what I wanted to do for the rest of my life. I had no clue what I would be good at and just fell into the first job I was offered at a bank, and I ended up staying there for the next thirty-six years. Things started out well for me, and I was successful in retail banking. I should have stayed there because I liked what I was doing and had a passion for interacting with customers and helping them with their financial lives. But I was swayed by the allure of commercial banking. That's where I thought all the successful and important people in the bank worked and I wanted to be just like them.

I jumped into commercial banking blindly, and that's when I started to stray off course. I ended up pursuing a path that I really didn't like, and I did it for all the wrong reasons—I did it for the professional success and status. I wanted to be a winner and make a lot of money, but truth be told, I wasn't meant to be in that position. It was a bad choice for me, as I was constantly working from my weaknesses instead of playing to my strengths, and it's hard to be happy when you are not doing what you like or are good at. I also learned a big lesson from working there: it's a huge mistake to trade in your authenticity just so you can fit in and be liked. It took me years to recover from that one!

Eventually I became a manager and had a team of account managers reporting to me. Most of them had their MBA, which didn't mean anything in the grand scheme of things, but it made me feel like a fraud; I felt I wasn't "good enough" due to my failure to secure a university degree. Not having a degree resulted in me suffering for years from low self-esteem. I was constantly worried about being found out, and this anxiety developed into a classic case of imposter syndrome. In spite of all the success I achieved, I always felt like a fraud, and believe me, it's not fun living like that.

The only way I could deal with my imposter syndrome was to win every sales contest I could, and I was quite successful at that; but over time it took a lot out of me. As the wins mounted up, at some point I grew indifferent to them. I would win the annual sales trip and not feel good about it at all. It felt like every time I won, I lost as well, if that makes any sense. Funny how fear works. But because of the way I was raised, I was stubborn and didn't know how to quit, which meant I was stuck in that job I didn't like for the duration.

I can't tell you how many times I checked my pension statement, recalculating how much more of my life I had to waste before the handcuffs would finally be off and I would be free. I felt that retirement was my only escape because my duty as a father was to protect my family by not losing my job. I didn't want to let my family down, but doing work I didn't like with people I didn't like forced me to find unhealthy ways of coping and decompressing. At the end of another stressful day, I would pop open a beer after dinner, collapse in front of the TV, and numb out. The shame of it all eroded my courage and faith in myself, but I didn't know what else to do but to suck it up and hang on and try to make it to the finish line.

Little did I know that when I got there and went back over all the years of work and conformity, I would find a new beginning.

Reviewing the movie of my life was the wake-up call I needed to reconnect with my childhood self, with the people I love, and with my zest for living. Seeing myself as if for the first time gave me a new start in retirement.

Questions for Self-Reflection

- What did you learn about yourself and your life after watching your movie?
- What makes you feel good about yourself?
- What were some of your biggest/favorite accomplishments?
- What activities over the past decades brought you the most joy?
- What makes you happy and lights you up?
- How do you like to spend your time?
- What can you do for hours without feeling bored? What activities put you in a state of flow?
- What are your positive qualities?
- What are some of the good things in your life?
- What are you good at? What comes easy to you?
- What brings you the greatest amount of joy?
- What do you love doing?
- What bothers you about your life? (e.g., job, marriage, health, family)
- What caused you to get sidetracked in your movie?
- What are you missing in your life that's preventing you from being happy?
- After watching your movie, do you have any regrets? Is there anything you can do to eliminate those regrets?
- Which of the problems in your life were caused by others? Which were caused by you?
- What are you embarrassed about?
- How would you rate your movie so far on a scale of 1–10?
- If you could live your life again after watching your movie and knowing what you know now, what would you do differently?

Simple Truths

- The seeds of a successful retirement are found in the movie of your earlier life.
- Your movie shows you who you were and gets you thinking about who you want to be and what you want to do.
- You are the author of your own life, so why wouldn't you write a good ending to your movie?
- To find your purpose you need increased self-awareness to figure out what is truly right for you.
- To achieve happiness and fulfillment in Victory Lap you need to become your true self.
- Learning from the past is vital for future success.
- Self-knowledge will help you move your life in the direction you want it to go.
- Once you realize who you really are and start making choices from that place, your retirement will turn around for the better.

14

Discovering Your Values

Your beliefs become your thoughts, your thoughts become your words, your words become your actions, your actions become your habits, your habits become your values, your values become your destiny.
—*Mahatma Gandhi*

It's important to understand that we are not all the same. We each have our own unique personal history as well as differing worldviews about retirement and about life in general, based on our own beliefs and biases. Because of this, we will all have differing "correct answers" about how our retirement should be lived. The key is to know yourself well, so you can choose the appropriate strategies that will work best for you.

To find your "correct answers," you need to have a good sense of who you are, what makes you happy, and what you need to do to make that happy happen. When you can match what you do daily with your values, you will enjoy an awesome retirement. Pretty simple when you think about it.

Values and Authenticity

Everyone has a different combination of core values that are as unique to them as their fingerprints. Your values represent the things that are most important to you. They influence your worldview, the choices that you make and how you behave. One of the biggest causes of stress and frustration for people is living a life that is "out of whack" with their values. They feel a disconnection from their authentic selves, which leads to a sense of discontent. They can sense in their gut that something is wrong, and they're frustrated because they're unhappy, but they just can't put their finger on what's making them feel that way. This can happen in retirement just as easily as it can at any other time, if you don't have a good sense of what really drives you.

But don't feel bad if you feel like this, because the truth is that few people clearly understand what their values are and what will make them happy in retirement. Instead, they default to allowing society and the media to tell them what they are supposed to want or value in their life after work, and the truth is that many times we want or need something different than what they tell us we need. We are told how successful retirees should look, how we should dress, what we should eat, what vacations we should go on, and which car we should drive.

It's a big mistake to get sucked into other people's values relating to retirement because what friends, family, colleagues, and those retirement commercials are telling you isn't necessarily realistic or right for you, and inside you know it.

You know the commercials I'm talking about: the happy, carefree couple sitting on a beach in the Caribbean drinking Corona or sailing on a yacht with the sun shining and the wind blowing through their full heads of beautiful white hair as they embrace each other, smiling with their brilliant, perfect smiles. The advertisers try to convince us that once we retire and stop working, our lives will automatically become better than before and we will be happier. This fantasy version of retirement has become so ingrained that it has become an expectation of society in general. This is what we think we're supposed to want. Seems logical, doesn't it? But for many retirees, the opposite is true. Full-stop retirement is not a natural act, and for people like me it's a bad move to retire to a life based solely on leisure when we might have another twenty or thirty years to go. Most of us need and want more.

It's time to stop pretending everything will be OK and that the same vision of retirement will work for everyone. It's time to open your eyes to the real retirement that *you* will be facing. Don't allow yourself to believe that you're a loser if you can't afford or don't want the advertisers' version of retirement. Do you really want to live the life that's portrayed in commercials about traditional retirement or to live other people's dreams? I sure don't!

One day you will wake up (hopefully you do wake up) to the fact that spending money just to buy things so you can feel good about yourself isn't such a good idea after all. Nor is living a retirement dream that's not your own or that's not aligned with your personal values. Simply going along with what you think retirement is supposed to look like comes at the cost of you losing touch with who you really are and, ultimately, your happiness.

How to Discover Your Values

Going through this exercise is often a wake-up call for people, as it makes them realize that many of the things they currently do are not necessarily aligned to their values. The fact is that values can change over time, and sometimes they evolve so gradually we are not even aware the change is happening. Before you know it, you've become someone you don't recognize, and what's driving you isn't really what turns your crank.

Values are formed starting in early childhood and are later consciously or subconsciously re-evaluated and changed as we transition through various stages of life. For example, when we went to work, we may have intentionally suppressed some of our values so we could fit in and focus on building our careers.

> Your core values are the deeply held beliefs that automatically describe your soul.
> —John Maxwell

We were willing to give up some of the things that were important to us and our sense of self-worth, just so we could make money. We were willing to compete with others, and our employers loved that about us. We competed to get the promotion so we could buy the big house, the fancy car, and all the other toys, believing that whoever made the most money and owned the most stuff was the worthiest.

When we got married and started a family, our values shifted again. Working hard, protecting our jobs, and taking care of our family became our top priorities rather than what was important to us individually. For example, if travel and adventure were top values for us in earlier years, we had to put them far on the back burner to make ends meet once we had kids and a big mortgage.

We all value our health, yet we are willing to reduce our time spent on health-improving activities such as working out, enjoying our hobbies, and spending quality time with friends so that we can instead save up for our kids' education or add some more money to the old retirement account. We end up losing sight of ourselves and what makes us happy because we are so focused on everyone else and the expectations others have of us, including society in general.

Later, after the kids grow up and leave to start out on their own, things change yet again. With the pressure off, we start to get a sense that something is wrong and that our current lifestyle is not in sync with our core values. Working hard for a company or a boss you don't like doesn't interest you anymore and starts rubbing you the wrong way, and that is when the trouble starts. You begin to wonder if this is all there is, and you may feel regret over priorities you shelved to put other people's needs and expectations first.

When you retire, what was once important to you while working will not be as important. You won't have to compete anymore, and you won't have to tolerate bullshit anymore. At this stage of life, meaning is no longer derived from who owns the biggest house, who drives the biggest car, or who makes the most money. Which is good, because we never did believe in those values anyway. To help you recognize what values do have meaning to you so that you can design a happy and fulfilling retirement, find a quiet place where you are alone and free from distractions and work through the steps we recommend in the following pages.

Step 1: Identifying Your Values—Listen to Your Heart, It's All About Feelings

To start the process of identifying your values, we need to go back to your movie and search for those peak moments in your life, the moments where you were willing to get out of your comfort zone and do something new and challenging. These moments are the experiences that you will never forget, the ones that change you, help you grow, and leave a mark on you. Examples of peak moments could be completing a marathon, doing your first big speech, winning a big award at work, or going on a trip to a place you have never been to before, like Thailand.

In your journal, list some of your peak experiences and then identify your values that were triggered or fulfilled by them. If you need help matching values to those experiences, just search "values" on Google and you will find an array of characteristics and qualities that you can choose from. Identifying your peak experiences and recognizing which of your values were satisfied through them should be a pretty easy exercise.

Next, go back to your movie and dig a little deeper. You now want to look at some of your past choices and figure out your "why" for making them. Our core values often influence the major life choices we make—or can be sacrificed in the process if we make a decision that conflicts with our values. Figuring out the "why" for doing what you have done over the years can help you identify your most fundamental personal values. So, think about why a particular choice was so important to you. Why did it make you feel so good or feel so bad? Now write down in your journal why some of your decisions made you happy and why some of them made you mad, sad, frustrated, or uncomfortable.

Your core values are closely tied to the major life decisions you make, influencing your choices and your happiness whether you're aware of it or not. If your choices are aligned with your personal values, you'll probably feel satisfied and fulfilled, generally speaking. However, if your decisions are not in alignment with your values, you are more likely to experience internal conflict, dissatisfaction, and unhappiness.

Do some soul-searching here to figure out the real reasons behind your key decisions and look for patterns over the years in the "why" for doing what you did. This process of self-examination will help you to identify your core values, whether you have been acting on them, or against them, subconsciously. Following, I offer examples of questions I've asked myself to help me determine what my values are.

Question: What do I love doing?
Answer: Fishing

What values of mine are reflected in that activity?
- health
- freedom
- adventure
- challenge
- privacy
- spirituality

Question: What makes me feel proud?
Answer: Writing a book

What values of mine are reflected in that activity?
- achievement
- financial prosperity
- concern for others

Question: What makes me angry? (Note: when you are angry there is a conflict with some of your values.)
Answer: Watching politicians lie on TV makes me angry.

What values of mine are being compromised by that deception?
- concern for others
- responsibility
- integrity
- honesty

Question: What is one of my favorite quotes?
Answer:

> *You can have everything in life you want if you will just help enough other people get what they want.*
>
> *—Zig Ziglar*

What values of mine are reflected in that quote?
- concern for others
- responsibility
- belonging

Questions for Self-Reflection
- What are you most proud of? (e.g., learning something new, awards won, relationships made)
- What aren't you happy about?
- What makes you angry?
- What are your passions? What makes you happy when you are doing it?
- What have you forced yourself to settle for? Why did you behave the way you did?
- What needs to change in your life in order for you to be happy?
- Which of your beliefs help you and which ones hinder you?
- What were five of your best decisions?
- What were five of your worst decisions?
- What are your strengths and weaknesses?
- What are you passionate/excited about?
- What negative thoughts from certain periods in your life constantly fill your mind? Why?
- What do you wish you hadn't given up doing?
- Where do you spend/invest your money?
- Who are your role models? Why?
- What is your favorite quote? Why?
- What movies inspire you? Why?
- What excites you to get out of bed in the morning?
- What do you wish you could have done?
- What were the "peak" moments in your movie?
- When was the last time you felt most passionate and alive?
- When were you lit up? When did time fly by?

Step 2: Prioritize Your Values

Make a list of the values you identified in your journal and then go over them one by one and select those that are most significant. When you read over your value list, see which ones make you experience a sense of excitement or passion. That tingly feeling you get inside when you think about them—those are the keepers.

Your "core" values are the ones that keep showing up on your list when you are answering your "why" questions. They are your strongest values, the ones that matter the most to you. Looking back at my sample list, one value that kept showing up was my concern for others, which is a top value of mine.

Questions for Self-Reflection
- Which values keep showing up on your list?
- Which values get you excited when you think about them?
- Which values are you most proud of?

Step 3: Rate How You Are Currently Living Your Core Values

Look at each of the core values you listed and assign a rating from 1–10 that is reflective of how often you satisfy, follow, or exhibit that value on a regular basis. What can you start doing today to get each rating to a 10?

Questions for Self-Reflection
- Which of your values are you acting on consistently?
- Where do you need to improve so that your actions and decisions are more consistent with your values? In other words, which values are you not living by on a regular basis?
- How satisfied are you that your values are aligned with your actions and decisions?

Value Conflicts: Good Values vs. Bad Habits

Were any of the values on your list negative ones? Or were you like most people and only put down the ones that made you feel good about yourself? More than likely, all the values you listed are noble and positive. But you may have found in the process of identifying and rating your values that you don't always act in accordance with them. Good values are no good at all if they are sublimated by bad habits and behaviors. Negative actions are the ones that embarrass and frustrate you because they are in direct conflict with your values. You know they are bad for you and will cost you long-term, but you engage in them anyway because they make you feel good or because that's what you think others expect of you.

After reviewing your movie a few times, you will have gained a sense of the values that are important to you as well as a sense of the self-sabotaging behaviors that have been holding you back from having a great life. In fact, you really didn't need to watch your movie, did you, because you always knew that some of what you were doing was harming you and going against what was truly important to you, but you did it anyway.

> Accept yourself, love yourself, and keep moving forward. If you want to fly, you have to give up what weighs you down.
>
> —Roy T. Bennett

In your journal, write out your bad habits and what you think they have cost you over the years in terms of your health and well-being. After you are finished with that, write down what you think will happen to you if you keep doing them.

Some examples of bad habits and behaviors that can undermine your personal values:

- eating too much crap
- drinking too much
- going to the casino every weekend
- spending too much time on social media
- watching too much TV
- gossiping to every person you meet

You can't make things better until you stop making things worse, and you can't enjoy a great Victory Lap until you stop doing the things that harm you or that work against your values and goals. You essentially have three options: you can eliminate the bad habit, you can reduce the number of times you practice the bad habit, or you can keep doing what you are doing and have a shitty retirement.

Let's use drinking beer as an example. I love beer, but having too much of it works against my core value of improving my health. I used to enjoy having a cold beer while barbequing in the summer after a hard day's work. Unfortunately, over the years, that preference of mine became a bad habit, compounding into some serious weight gain. Gradually, that one beer led to two or three, and after having a few beers I would bail on my planned after-dinner walk with the Contessa and just slump in front of the TV to numb out for a few hours before going to bed.

So why did I drink all those beers knowing that it would usually end up with me missing out on a nice walk with the Contessa and that this habit was negatively affecting my health? It's because my health at that point in time was not one of my top values. I might have thought it was, but it really wasn't. In the moment, I was ranking the short-term enjoyment of drinking a cold beer (or several of them) over my stated personal value of good health, because that cold beer made me feel good and helped take the edge off.

The worst part was, every time I caved, I would feel guilty knowing that what I was doing was bad for my health, but I couldn't stop myself. There is nothing worse than betraying yourself again and again. That leads to serious internal conflict and horrible feelings of guilt. You end up feeling like a loser because you know that what you are doing is hurting you.

In order to fix things and eliminate the stress generated from this value conflict, I needed to either change the hierarchy of my good-health value vis-à-vis my beer-drinking habit or eliminate my beer-drinking habit completely, which would not be an easy thing to do because I still enjoyed having a cold beer.

To help motivate me to make the required change, I asked myself the following questions:

- What is it costing me in terms of my health to hold on to my current habit of drinking beer every night?
- What kind of conflict will I continue to experience as a result of holding on to this habit, which works directly against the value I place on good health?

After answering these questions, it was easy to see that the short-term costs and long-term consequences of maintaining my daily beer-drinking habit were unacceptable. The trade-off between drinking cold beer every night and living a shorter, lower-quality life was not a good one, and knowing this made the process of changing that habit easier for me. I didn't end up eliminating my beer-drinking completely; but I did prioritize my health over the short-term satisfaction of having a beer, which means I still enjoy a cold beer from time to time, just much less often than I did before.

As the Roy T. Bennett quote on page 180 says, remember to be kind to yourself in the process of identifying your bad habits that are in conflict with your values and while working toward making them less of a priority than your core values. Being too hard on yourself will only make you feel more guilty, and to comfort yourself, you may risk falling back into the very habits you're trying to reduce or eliminate. Focus on the positive values you've identified and on putting them first—before the bad habits that get in the way of fulfilling them.

> When your values are clear to you, making decisions becomes easier.
> —Roy E. Disney

Just remember that putting your values first influences your decisions; and how you choose to act and behave will ultimately determine your sense of happiness and fulfillment. Living your values is fundamental to finding the Retirement Heaven you are seeking.

The Nine Retirement Principles and Your Values

If you have been paying attention, you will have noticed that the nine retirement principles outlined in Part 2 mirror many of the core values that you identified for yourself. They are likely fairly consistent with the things that are most important to you. This is an important relationship because if the principles didn't match up well with your values and beliefs, you would struggle trying to live up to them. It's impossible to motivate yourself to do something even when it's good for you when you don't believe in what you are doing.

Using Your Values to Help Find Your Purpose

Because you now know your core values, you know what is most important to you and you can use that understanding to help you figure out how you want to spend your remaining time, and what you need to do to be fulfilled. Will sitting on a couch eating potato chips while watching TV satisfy your values and make you happy, or do you need to find something more fulfilling to do?

Use your values to help you find your purpose—something you can enjoy doing every day; something that will bring you joy every time you do it; something that will give you a sense of personal satisfaction. It might be something you can play at and get lost in again, or it could be a way to help others. Whatever it is that satisfies your sense of purpose.

LESSONS FROM A PANDEMIC

Our most basic instinct is not for survival but for family. Most of us would give our own life for the survival of a family member, yet we lead our daily life too often as if we take our family for granted.

—*Paul Pearsall*

The COVID-19 pandemic taught us what "cabin fever" truly feels like, and experiencing that fever created a short-term internal conflict for many people. Core values like eating healthy and exercising took a back seat to some bad habits for a while. Folks started to spend too much time watching TV, allowing useless activities to consume most of their day and drinking way more than they should. And who could blame them? Life was pretty upside down for a period of time. But eventually most people woke up to what was happening to them. Their good values started to bubble to the surface and they were able to get back on track.

What I found interesting was the reprioritization of some of our most fundamental values. Relationships with people went to the top of everyone's list, along with a concern for our health. The pandemic heightened our awareness of what really mattered and reminded us of what was genuinely important in our lives. When times were tough, you wanted your loved ones around you for comfort, company and security during a challenging time. Sadly, because some of us were so busy with other things before the crisis, we had forgotten that.

During the pandemic, we remembered who our real friends were as we reached out to them and they reached out to us to check on one another. We were reminded that it didn't take a lot of money to survive. In fact, having a lot of money didn't do a person a lot of good, because there weren't many places to spend it. As long as you could put food on the table and buy the necessities like groceries, toilet paper, and hand sanitizer, you were OK. We were all in the same boat, trying to survive. Designer clothes, expensive jewelery, and driving a fancy car held little value during the pandemic. The things we really valued were a good meal, good company, and a safe place to live.

My Story

Going through the value discovery exercise was a big wake-up call for me. I had never thought about the values–happiness connection before, and it made me realize that many of the things that I did and/or put up with in my past working life did not align with my core values. Now I know why I felt so frustrated and stressed out for all those years.

Like most kids growing up, some of my values were culturally influenced. In my case, it was often through watching movies, and John Wayne and Clint Eastwood were my heroes and role models. I loved the code they lived by, and I intentionally adopted some of their values to be more like them. My heroes taught me to be tenacious and never give up. To be tough and stoic like they were, and to never show emotion or how you were really feeling. To go it alone and never ask for help, because asking for help was a sign of weakness and vulnerability. They also taught me the importance of honesty, integrity, honor, respect, and trust, which continue to be big values of mine to this day.

Because of my cowboy values, I never indulged in company politics, ass-kissing, or blowing my own horn, and I'm thankful for that. But when I went to work in the Corp, I had to suppress some of my values so I wouldn't get into trouble, and doing that caused me a lot of stress over the years. When I had been younger, I always felt the need to speak up when I saw something was wrong, and I did that early in my career; but things changed when I had a family and needed to protect my job. It felt wrong to be silent and not do the right thing, but all I could do was withdraw and keep my opinions to myself. I will always regret the times I forced myself to pretend everything was all right when it wasn't. Out of necessity, in my working life I changed the hierarchy of my values and added some new ones. My top-three values became achievement, status, and competition so I could keep my job and provide security for my family. I did well in my job, and it paid me well, but it was slowly killing me because it didn't match up with who I really was.

Another big problem for me was always going it alone and not asking for help, which only contributed to my imposter syndrome. I tried to figure everything out for myself, although I often felt like a fraud and unworthy. Because I was tenacious and wouldn't give up, I made it almost to the finish line. But it did come at a cost—the cost of my well-being.

One day after leaving the bank, I took one of those assessment tests to see if I was a good candidate to start my own business, and I wasn't surprised when I scored twenty out of twenty—a perfect score. The test confirmed my need for a high degree of autonomy, something that rubbed off on me after watching all those John Wayne movies. I really don't like being told what to do, especially by someone whom I don't respect, and historically there has always been a strong correlation between my degree of autonomy and my performance. Whenever I had a boss who trusted me and gave me a lot of rope, I would "outperform"; but give me a boss who micromanaged me, and my performance would be average at best because it went against my core value.

Since starting my Victory Lap, I've worked hard at changing some of my old cowboy values that were getting in my way and holding me back. Asking for help is no longer a weakness of mine, and I'm no longer concerned about showing my emotions and letting people know how I feel inside. Every once in a while, usually after watching a good movie or seeing something that moves me, I tear up. I know it's not very "John Wayney," but I'm kind of proud that I can now do that.

Questions for Self-Reflection
- Are your values and your retirement in sync?
- Do you share the same values as your spouse?
- Were there any surprises when you created your list of values?
- Do some of the values you listed cause you any concern?
- Are there some values higher/lower on the list than you expected?
- How well are you currently living the values you listed? Are you satisfying what is most important to you?
- Are you making value-based decisions?
- What are your roadblocks, your bad habits, the things that get in the way of you hitting your values on a regular basis?
- What are some real-life consequences that will happen if you do not change your bad habits?
- Is there a disconnect between how you spend your time and money and your core values?
- Why do you do things that will bother you and harm you?
- What will you choose to no longer do?

Simple Truths
- Retirement is so much easier when we know what our values are and how to satisfy them.
- Values are who you are even when no one is watching.
- Putting your values first influences your decisions; and how you choose to act and behave will ultimately determine your sense of happiness and fulfillment in life.
- Boredom is a warning sign that you are not hitting your values.
- Living a life that is inauthentic—out of alignment with your values—drains your energy and will take a major toll on you over time.

- Happiness is the joy we feel as we grow toward who we're supposed to be.
- Once you have a good handle on your values, finding your purpose in life becomes much easier.
- When you know what your values are and can find a way to satisfy those values, you will experience a sense of fulfillment.
- Real fulfillment doesn't come from having a lot of money and material possessions; it comes from finding out what makes you happy and brings you joy, and then doing those things.

15

Finding Meaningful Work

For, in the end, it is impossible to have a great life unless it is a meaningful life. And it is very difficult to have a meaningful life without meaningful work.
—James C. Collins

What I've learned after talking to thousands of people at our seminars, via our blog, and at the Zoomer retirement shows in Toronto is that few people of traditional retirement age want to stop working completely. They might want to spend less time working or do a different kind of work than they did in their full-time primary career, but they still want to be involved in something. And what I learned is backed up by AARP (American Association of Retired Persons), which has reported that more than 50 percent of retired persons would rather be working.

The traditional image of retirement—the one we often see in the media and in advertisements—conveys the message that we shouldn't work anymore and that we shouldn't even want to. It's all about relaxing and living a life of leisure. But this rubs some of us the wrong way because we know that it's the wrong message for us. As we saw in Part 2 and elsewhere in the book, having a purpose, making a contribution, and mattering to others is still just as important to us in retirement as it is during the career years.

When you leave the world of full-time work, you could lose a lot, and it's not just all about the money. You may experience Sudden Retirement Shock when you lose any or all of the following:

- your primary reason for getting out of bed in the morning
- satisfaction derived by accomplishing a goal
- feelings of importance and knowing that you matter
- self-esteem and respect from your bosses, co-workers, and customers
- status
- your sense of identity
- companionship and camaraderie
- a daily consistent routine/structure to follow
- a source of active income
- a way of satisfying your innate needs

For many of us, work gave us a core sense of who we were. It was a big part of our identity and our social world, and going to work made us happy, challenged, and fulfilled. Our work fed our innate needs and was a major part of satisfying our core values. When we leave full-time work behind, we become separated from what was meaningful to us, we lose our purpose, and that is when the depression sets in. The bottom line is that, if not planned and managed properly, the transition to retirement can be a living hell. So, why let this happen to you if you don't have to?

The New Retirement: Working in Your Victory Lap

We need to take a new approach to retirement and how it should be lived because, as we now know, retiring to nothing is associated with early death, diminishing health, expanding boredom, and high rates of divorce. Work can be a big part of remaining happy, healthy, and fulfilled in retirement. (That's one reason we like to refer to this exciting new stage of your life as Victory Lap rather than retirement.) At this point, work doesn't have to mean career, and it certainly doesn't have to be full-time. It may not even be the same as the work you were doing when you were employed at the Corp. In fact, when I refer to work, it doesn't even have to be paid work. Unpaid work such as volunteering for a special cause or being part of a committee can provide the same benefits as paid work except for the money part.

According to the Pew Research Center, more and more workers are retiring later than they have in the past. Between 2004 and 2014, the number of Americans at least fifty-five years old who were active in the labor force grew by 47.1 percent. That number is expected to grow nearly 20 percent over the next ten years, and workers over the age of fifty-five are expected to be 25 percent of the labor market by 2024. The facts point to a growing trend: more people are working longer, either because they need to or because they want to.

Working Because You Need To

Unless you have managed to save up a bunch of money over the years, traditional full-stop retirement is pure fantasy for many hard-working people. In other words, many of us will *need* to keep working. Period. There is no other option. I know that sounds harsh, but it's the simple truth. Some people will *need* to work for as long as they are healthy, to support the retirement lifestyle they want.

You might not be aware of this, but when you examine income data from both the United States and Canada, it's easy to see that many people can't afford to both live a typical middle-class lifestyle in their working years and save enough to finance a retirement that will last twenty years or more. Traditional retirement was designed for much shorter lifespans, and that financial reality is causing a lot of stress for people.

In fact, a report put out by the Insured Retirement Institute entitled "Boomer Expectations For Retirement 2019" stated that in the United States, 45 percent of boomers have zero savings for retirement. Unfortunately, the situation is similar in Canada. This means traditional full-stop retirement in North America is little more than a pipe dream for many hard-working people. Sure, some retirees will try to get by solely on Social Security in the United States (CPP and OAS in Canada), but that would be a big mistake because of the effect of inflation on things such as rent, property taxes, food, and health care spending.

Talk about being in Retirement Hell, where every year you live is a little worse than the one before. Every passing year, your retirement world would become smaller and smaller in terms of what you can afford to do. Money would be tight and getting tighter, your stress would keep going up, and sadly, you may not even be able to do things like visit your kids at Christmas if they live on the other side of the country and you can't afford the price of a plane ticket.

Living a retirement like that sucks, there is no other word for it. So, our advice to you is that if you are healthy enough to work, get out there—find some good work for yourself, or preferably great work (more on the difference between those two later), to supplement your income and give you a renewed sense of purpose.

If you find yourself in a situation where your retirement savings are insufficient to support the lifestyle you want, you face three basic choices:

1. Keep working at your full-time job for a few years longer than you planned so you can build up enough savings to cover your spending needs in retirement.
2. Cut your expenses in retirement (which means cutting back the lifestyle you envisioned) so you can live within your means.
3. Work just enough in retirement, at something you enjoy, to help subsidize the life you've dreamed of.

And a word of caution here: You probably shouldn't consider full-stop retirement at all if you fit any of the following criteria. Don't retire if:

- you have a lot of debt,
- you have limited retirement savings,
- you have nothing interesting to do, and/or
- your only friend is the TV.

Working Because You Want To

As we've seen earlier in this chapter and elsewhere in the book, there are many benefits to continuing to work in retirement, at least in some way and to some degree. Lots of research has proven that working later in life helps people stay healthy and engaged. As you'll see below, working in some capacity in your Victory Lap can help you practice many of the nine retirement principles, in addition to providing you with some fun money to enjoy your life to the max.

> To find joy in work is to discover the fountain of youth.
> —Pearl S. Buck

The Benefits of Continuing to Work

- Work—the right work—should be fun and make you happy. Work is right when it fulfills many of your values and enriches your life. When you can satisfy your values and needs through your work, life is pretty good, so why would you ever want to retire from something you love to do? (Retirement Principle #9)
- Work will help you live longer. Studies have shown that people who continue to labor on in retirement have fewer health problems and live longer lives than retirees who end up watching too much TV, don't exercise, and lack ways to keep their minds sharp. As described in a 2019 *Wall Street Journal* article, "The Case Against Early Retirement," researchers for the Center for Retirement Research at Boston College found that delaying retirement reduced the five-year mortality risk for men in their early sixties by 32 percent. (Retirement Principle #2)
- Retiring results in a loss of camaraderie that working provided. By continuing to work, you will avoid becoming socially isolated, which we know is not a good thing. (Retirement Principle #1)
- Retiring to do nothing, or full-stop retirement as we call it, can accelerate cognitive decline. Work keeps you sharp, requiring you to learn new skills and solve problems, which keeps the brain healthy. Playing bridge or doing crossword puzzles simply is not as intellectually challenging as work is. (Retirement Principle #2)
- Work provides a continuing source of active income, which reduces the stress from worrying that you will run out of money in retirement. Having some money coming in, even on a scaled-back basis, allows you to better weather difficult times (think, a pandemic or a financial

market meltdown) and increases your financial options to make the most of your assets as a retiree (for example, deferring drawing down on your retirement portfolio in a declining market or putting off claiming government pensions to create a bigger guaranteed benefit in the future). (Retirement Principle #3)

- Maintaining some degree of earned income gives parents the freedom to help their kids and grandkids without jeopardizing their own retirement (for example, supporting their kids who had lost their jobs in the COVID-19 pandemic, or helping to finance the grandkids' education). (Retirement Principle #1)
- Work gives you purpose—a good reason to get out of bed in the morning—and will shield you from boredom. (Retirement Principle #9)

Preparing to Work in Retirement

Most retirees have some kind of financial cushion and their cash flow needs are lower after the kids have gone and the mortgage has been paid off. You may even be financially independent at this point in your life, with enough income and investments to cover your essential expenses. Either way, not being stressed financially means you do not have to make money right out of the gate. You can be patient and take your time to find meaningful work or even build a successful business of your own.

A good part of the rest of this chapter is focused on preparing for your job search and helping you find or create the right type of work for you. It's impossible to cover everything you need to know in a single chapter, so if you need more information relating to job hunting, we recommend you read *What Color Is Your Parachute? A Practical Manual for Job-Hunters and Career-Changers* by Richard N. Bolles, which is full of great advice and tactics. Also, if you are interested in starting your own business, we recommend reading *WISER: The Definitive Guide to Starting a Business after the Age of 50*, by Wendy Mayhew. The book contains thoughts and advice from leading experts on all the different activities that are necessary in order to launch a business successfully later in life.

Facing Your Fear

I'm not going to lie to you, looking for work at this point in your life can be uncomfortable, and it's even harder if you were pushed out the door from your full-time career. Looking for a new job causes your inner gremlin to come out, as you will be exposed to fears that you haven't experienced for a long time: the fear of rejection, of not being good enough, of being seen as too old, of having to convince someone much younger than you to hire you, and of starting over at something new and being afraid that you are too old to learn new things.

It's natural to be afraid at this stage of the game, but it's not OK to allow your inner gremlin to keep you from doing what you need or want to do. You need to believe in yourself. The truth is that you are more than capable. You're experienced and have proven yourself many times before, you just haven't been tested for a while.

Getting Your Confidence Back

A good way to get your confidence back is to make a list of your past accomplishments. Think back to times when you were excited and scared but still succeeded in accomplishing something great. Remember when you landed your first job offer or when you won the annual sales contest, got the promotion you wanted, or did your first speech and received a big ovation? Your list will both surprise you and boost your self-esteem as you remember how good you really are when you want something bad enough. It's important to understand that what you are planning to do in Victory Lap Retirement is nothing compared to what you have already accomplished in your past working life.

Another way to reflect on your achievements is to go through the exercise of decluttering, which the Contessa and I did when we were preparing for some significant renovations at home. We were forced to go through all the stuff that we had accumulated over the years, and that process made us think a lot about our past life. When you pick up something in a room among the old sports trophies, finisher medals, books, work awards, report cards, photos, clothes, and other artifacts and you start the "Should I keep or toss?" decision-making process, your mind is flooded with old memories. You remember all your past accomplishments you had forgotten about, the wins you worked so hard for. You can still feel the excitement you experienced when you committed, went "all in" on something, and got it done. It's all there, what you were capable of at work and outside of it, and as you go through things you suddenly remember how tough and capable you really are. You will realize you still have more wins within you and that you are far from done yet.

Finding the Right Work to Fulfill Your Needs

After working for twenty or thirty years or more, hopefully you know yourself pretty well and have a good handle on what type of work you find interesting. Remember, in the Victory Lap phase it doesn't have to be the same work you were doing in your career; and if it is, it doesn't have to be to the same extent. You could do something completely different, work only part-time, or even volunteer your time. The point is that you want to choose work that is meaningful to you, gives you purpose, matches your core values, and plays to your special talents.

For instance, if you value your autonomy, working in an office job might not be a good fit for you. If you value connection, interaction, and friendship, working alone at home writing a novel is not the way to go for you. If you like to travel and meet new people and you enjoy selling something that people need, a traveling sales job might be perfect for you.

If you're not immediately sure what kind of work you might do in your Victory Lap, look at your past work experience and make a list of the strengths and skills that made you a valuable employee. It can also be helpful to get outside opinions, so consider asking your friends or former work colleagues what they think you bring to the table—why you are a winner. Identifying your strengths might give you some ideas of what to pursue next.

It's also a good idea to use some of the free self-assessment quizzes online, at Careerpath.com and Monster.com, for example, to see how your perceived list of strengths and skills lines up with their test results. These quizzes can even help heighten awareness of your own strengths. If you are really good at something or some kind of work comes easily to you, you could be taking your strengths for granted, forgetting that you are uniquely equipped with certain skills and talents. The assessments will make you aware of this and might even give you some additional ideas for what work you would like to pursue.

Not long ago, I completed a self-assessment myself to determine if I would be suitable for self-employment. I scored a straight twenty out of twenty on the assessment, which was an eye-opener for me. I had never given self-employment much thought in the past but always knew deep down that I had a strong need for autonomy.

Another time, I decided to take a free personality test at 16Personalities.com, which confirmed some things I already knew about myself, but it also revealed that I would be a good coach or teacher. This was something I had never considered before and hadn't included on my list of skills and talents, but it made a lot of sense to me. I managed people in my bank job. The company had invested a lot of money over the years training me to be a coach, and I was good at it. While my commercial banking career wasn't the best fit for me, it did give me a lot of skills and experience that I could put to good use to create a successful Victory Lap. That is why these self-assessments are so important. They can open your eyes to things about yourself that you may not have otherwise seen. Maybe you will uncover some of your hidden talents, like I did.

LESSONS FROM A PANDEMIC

During the COVID-19 lockdown, people who couldn't work from home weren't able to work at all. Many who found themselves in that boat felt restless and bored and had no idea of what to do each day. Many couldn't wait to get back to the office. But many of those who worked from home during the pandemic woke up to the possibilities and benefits of having a home-based business. They learned that having a computer and an internet connection would allow them to work past normal retirement age doing something that they enjoy. They became confident they could be their own boss and consult, teach, blog, host webinars, or what have you right out of the comfort of their own home.

Like most people, during your career you probably sought new jobs and promotions so you could make more money. This type of thinking changes in Victory Lap, though; when you are financially independent (or close to it), the focus changes from pursuing money to pursuing work that gives you purpose and makes you happy. What most of us are looking for at this stage is part-time or seasonal work, or even volunteer work, so that we can reduce the stress in our lives and free up time for the other things that are important to us, such as our friends and family, eldercare, working out, leisure activities, and traveling. If you choose to work in retirement, you probably will not earn as much money as you did before, but that's OK because in Victory Lap you are focused not on how much money you make but on work that you enjoy and will give you the flexibility that you crave.

One of the most common job interview questions that older workers encounter is, "Why would someone with so much experience want this job?" You can read this another way as meaning, why would you be willing to do work and be paid less? Personally, I believe it's OK to say you see the purpose of work differently at this point in your life. You now know that working will keep you healthy both mentally and physically. So, unlike before, money is no longer the main motivator for you, nor is status or job titles.

You want a job where you can continue to be engaged, to learn, and to grow, but one that is less stressful. You want a job close to home so you can avoid a long commute. You want a job that is interesting, where you are working for a cause you believe in. At this stage of life, it's important for you to find work that you enjoy, a place where you can contribute. And in order for you to get that, you are willing to step back in terms of title and compensation because those other things are more important to you right now.

Questions for Self-Reflection
- What were your biggest successes in your working life?
- What were your biggest challenges/obstacles? How did you get past them?
- What skills have you developed? What have you learned about yourself?
- What are your strengths? What are your weaknesses?

- What weaknesses do you have that could be turned into strengths?
- What do you need to do to close the gap between where you are now and where you need to be?

Refuse to Let Ageism Get You Down

Don't use ageism as an excuse before you even start. I've hired a lot of older people in my day, and the reason I hired them was that they had a proven track record of being able to do the job. What I've learned is that age does not determine how well someone can do a job. In fact, many times age helps.

Understand the older worker's competitive advantage:

1. It's easier to get part-time, temp, and contract work because you are cheaper and not on the full-time payroll. A lot of companies today are outsourcing and using freelancers.

2. If you have financial independence, you don't really need a contract at this stage of the game. Show your willingness to work in a less-than-conventional way, and you will be more marketable.

3. You have been battle-tested and have a great deal of accumulated knowledge and experience. Unlike younger workers, you can hit the ground running and do the required work without training. Companies like the fact that you earn your money from day one.

4. There is a growing talent shortage because the boomers are starting to retire. Organizations are now courting older workers, in part to compensate for the skills shortage caused by the baby boomers retiring, but also in recognition of their wisdom, experience, ability to mentor younger workers, and proven management skills.

Update and Highlight Your Skills

Currently, one in three fifty-five-to-sixty-year-olds lack adequate technology skills, and hiring managers know this and will be asking about it. If you're part of that one-third, you need to get yourself up to speed with the technology tools you will be using before going on a job interview. Hiring people love to hear that you took some courses to update your skills in preparation for a new job. It shows initiative and makes you more attractive.

Some recruiters wrongly equate brains, energy, and the ability to think innovatively with youth. They wrongly believe that older workers are less technically savvy and that they lack stamina. You will get no favors from people who think like this, and therefore you will need to show that you have the right skills, attitudes, and know-how that qualify you as the "best person" for the job. To be the best, you should look for work that matches up well with your most important values and skills and talents; work that you like and will put you in the zone.

Remember, They Will Be Googling You

Depending on the job you are after, chances are good that your potential employers will conduct a google search on you, so make sure you have a good online presence such as a current LinkedIn profile. If you don't know how to do it, have someone create it for you. Also be aware that any viewable photos and information on your social media accounts (Facebook, Twitter, and others) contribute to how potential employers view you. So be sure to put in private mode any content that might compromise how you want potential employers to see you.

Image and Attitude Matter

You have only one shot at making a good first impression, and that first impression will stick in the mind of whoever is interviewing you. Everything from your hair to your shoes sends a message and is an indicator of who you are. The good news is that your clothes, your attitude, the way you talk, your body language, your energy level, and your confidence are all within your control, so in these ways you can make sure you are sending the right message. Dress like a winner, act like a winner, and odds are you will be a winner.

No one wants to hire a stiff—someone who doesn't fit in and isn't hungry. When you speak, you want to first show that you have some smarts and that you want to be there. Show them you are fun and kind, loyal, proud, dependable, trustworthy, a team player, and that you care. These are the qualities that hiring managers are looking for.

Be Willing to Explain What Happened

A lot of people get packaged these days for business reasons and if that's what happened to you, hiring managers will know it wasn't your fault, so don't be embarrassed about telling them you were let go. Reinforce your message of being a seasoned and veteran worker that they will benefit from hiring.

Hiring managers will want to know that you are fully committed to this new opportunity and so they will ask why you didn't pursue a new job right away. You can safely answer this question by saying that you spent time volunteering, tried writing a book, or provided eldercare. They would love hearing that you decided to take some time off to recharge and polish up on some of your skills before getting back in the game again so you could give it your best shot. Tell them about your interest in their company and what they do. (Hint: you should know this before you go on the interview.) Show them that you are excited about being a part of that. Give them some good reasons for choosing you.

Use the Power of Your Network

Most people get jobs through referrals, not by responding to job ads. With this in mind:

- Try to connect with people who would know how well you would do the work you are applying for.
- It's always easier to get hired if someone will vouch for you. For example, someone you worked with in the past who is now with the organization you want to work for.

Different Ways to Work in Victory Lap

One of the most common mistakes people make is to immediately jump into a job doing the same work they did before. While this may be the instinctive thing to do, it doesn't make a lot of sense going back to a job that you were counting the days to escape from. Nor should you make the same mistake that I did the first time around and jump into the first job you find. Best to take a break, regroup, and start searching for a better alternative. You have the time and freedom to choose what you want to do next, so avoid rushing and making a bad decision. Life is too short to be stuck in a job doing work that you don't enjoy. Discover what you are good at and what you are passionate about and pursue jobs in those areas. Do not restrict your search to your old industry.

Here are some tips for seeking work:

- Look at small companies and start-ups that can't afford full-time workers.
- Think about getting multiple income streams from a few small jobs.
- Build your network before you leave your primary career.
- Find environments where your skills and know-how will have an impact.
- Present yourself as a valuable mentor.

Staying with Your Current Employer

Not a lot of employers currently offer the option of letting you transition into part-time work, but you never know until you ask. Start talking with your boss as you near your retirement date. See if there are any opportunities for you to help out somewhere, perhaps as a part-time mentor or maybe as a trouble shooter. Companies, especially smaller ones, hate to lose good people and will bend over backwards trying to find a way to make things work out.

Buying an Existing Business

If you want to be your own boss, buying a business can be easier and less risky than starting one from scratch; but you have to go into it with both eyes open and understand the risks. It is important to consider why the business is being sold in the first place, whether there are any potential skeletons in the closet. You need to ask yourself if the business is really worth it, both in terms of monetary investment and in terms of the time that you will have to spend running it. This is why it's so critical to have a thorough understanding of your values and what you hope to achieve in your Victory Lap.

Buying a Franchise

There are some good franchises out there and buying a franchise is easier and less risky than launching your own business, but you will still need to put a lot of time in, and some require major financial investment. Another potential downside is that you have limited autonomy because you have to follow what the franchisor says.

Starting Your Own Business

Going to work for someone else on a part-time basis is far easier than starting your own business from scratch, but if you're having a hard time finding suitable work or you simply don't want to work for anyone else ever again, starting your own business is a good way to go, and many boomers are doing exactly that.

It's interesting to see that most boomers are not starting businesses in retirement just because they need the income. A 2015 Gallup Poll showed that eight out of ten boomer entrepreneurs started businesses for lifestyle reasons rather than financial ones. For boomer women, the top reason for going into business for themselves was the desire to pursue their passion, while boomer men were happy to finally be their own boss and to not have to take orders from someone else. And things are working out for these new business owners, as the average boomer business owner ranks their happiness at 8 on a scale of 1–10, with 10 being the happiest.

Starting a small business has become more possible than ever. Changes in the economy have led to more and more companies outsourcing services, making it the perfect time for small businesses to develop to fulfill those needs. And boomers are starting to catch on.

> If you build it, [they] will come.
>
> —Field of Dreams

This is a perfect opportunity for them to engage in work they want to do—on their terms.

- A 2016 US study conducted by the Kauffmann Foundation (Index of Startup Activity) found that 24.3 percent of all new entrepreneurs fell between the ages of fifty-five and sixty-four.
- In Canada, a 2019 TD Canada Trust survey found that 54 percent of baby boomers have started or considered starting a small business prior to retirement. The same study also found that 40 percent of workers over sixty-five are self-employed.

- A 2016 study from the UK's Office for National Statistics, "Five facts about . . . older people at work," found that 60 percent of workers aged seventy and older in the United Kingdom are self-employed.

And if you think you couldn't compete against a younger person when opening a business, you would be wrong. A fifty-year-old founder is 2.8 times more likely to start up a successful business than a twenty-five-year-old, according to a report titled "How Old Are Successful Tech Entrepreneurs?" by the Kellogg School of Management at Northwestern University. Older entrepreneurs have a big advantage over younger people when starting a business—and it basically comes down to experience.

Your Experience Is an Advantage

You've accumulated an extensive amount of knowledge and real-life experience over the years and have had the time to hone your skills. You have seen firsthand what works and what doesn't. This past experience will reduce the risk of you making any costly mistakes. Another benefit is that you can leverage the strong business network you've built up over the years. When you encounter a problem (and you will), you know exactly who to call to help out. Having the benefit of a large network gives you a big leg up in the entrepreneurial world, and a lot of millennials just haven't lived long enough to attain that yet.

Still scared about starting your own business? You shouldn't be. Consider this:

- The affordability and availability of technology means a person can start a business from anywhere there is a good internet connection. They can "retire" near the kids or on the beach and still start and run a business.

- It is cheaper and easier than ever before to launch a business.
- You can sub-contract things you are not very good at or do not want to do. There are companies that will help you do everything you can't or don't want to do, like building your website, setting up your PayPal account, filing your tax returns—whatever you need to have done. Help is out there; all you have to do is ask.
- Having a safety net in place is smart. For example, building up your new business while your spouse/partner continues working allows you to rely on her/his income until your new venture starts producing positive cash flow. And don't be surprised if that takes a while. Like they say, Rome wasn't built in a day!

To Make It Easier, Consider Partnering Up

One important lesson I learned while starting up my own business was that it's a mistake to try to do everything yourself. For instance, I suck with technology, but I'm good at public speaking, writing, and coaching. I realized that it was dumb to waste valuable time trying to learn something that I will never like doing when I could avoid all that pain by either outsourcing some of the tasks that I'm bad at or by partnering up with someone who knew what they were doing.

One of the smartest things I did was to team up with my partner, Gerry, as he can speak computer and handles all that tech stuff that I'm neither good at nor have an interest in learning. Teaming up allows me to play to my strengths, and that makes me happy. Because of Gerry I have less stress and more fun—and that, my friends, is what your Victory Lap should be all about.

Some of you might be reluctant to give up a part of your new business (it's human nature), but just remember that 100 percent of nothing is nothing while 50 percent of something is something. Why go it alone when there is a better, easier way by partnering up with someone?

Don't Settle for "Bad Work"

"Bad work" is work you hate but you are forced to do just to get by or to provide for some small lifestyle extras like joining a gym and going out for dinner once a month. Anyone can make money doing all kinds of distasteful things, but why would you when you have a choice? Working by standing on your feet all day dressed up in a chicken costume at the local chicken wing establishment just so you can survive is like being in prison. Bad work drains you and makes you feel inadequate, that you are not good enough, and thinking like that will lead to increased anxiety, disconnection, and a feeling of emptiness. Doing bad work usually leads to numbing—finding a way to decompress after the end of another shitty day. And we don't want to live like that anymore, do we?

Below is a list of examples of bad work that is specific to me based on my own values; but remember that just because it is bad work for me doesn't mean it would be bad work for you. For instance, bad work for me means it lacks autonomy, but some people want to be told what to do.

Examples of bad work that I need to avoid:

- work where I have to pretend to be someone else
- work that requires I sell a product I don't believe in
- work where I have to pressure people in order to make a sale
- work with competitive, selfish, unfriendly people
- work that comes with a bad boss or a bad company
- work where I'm micromanaged
- work that requires a brutal commute
- work where I have limited autonomy

Bottom line: It's hard to be happy if you're not doing work you like. Doing bad work will just make you feel bad. There are better things out there for you if you are willing to look for them.

Find Good Work

Good work is work that satisfies a number of your values; work that makes you feel good inside; work that you are good at and enjoy doing. It can be in a different job than you did before, or it can be in a less demanding role that is less taxing than your old job.

An example of good work for me might be working at Bass Pro Shops. I love fishing and talking about fishing, so working there would be a lot of fun for me. And because I have a great deal of passion for fishing, I'm confident I would be their best salesperson in that particular department. Although working there would be a good fit for me, I passed on the opportunity because a retail job like that wouldn't give me the autonomy, flexibility, and challenge I need that are other key values of mine. The best solution for me was to be patient and find/create "great work" for myself.

Finding Great Work: Pursuing Your Art

It's important to understand the distinction between good work and great work. Good work will give you the money you need and make you happy by satisfying some of your values, but great work will take your relationship with work to a much higher level. Great work is the payoff from figuring out why you were put on this planet (your mission). It's work that makes you come alive doing the thing you love to do, where you can cultivate the special gifts you were given and share them with the world. Finding great work is equivalent to finding your art, a subject that Seth Godin has written extensively about.

In this context, don't think of art literally, as being limited to only a painting or a sculpture or some other artistic object. Art is anything creative that you love so much you get lost in; any pursuit or type of work that you're passionate about. Art is personal and it's done on your own terms; often, it involves doing something that you feel is your way of contributing and making a difference. Finding your art is not so much about making money, it's more about how it makes you feel while making or doing it. It's a way of expressing who you are and

> If you are working on something exciting that you really care about, you don't have to be pushed. The vision pulls you.
>
> —Steve Jobs

what you believe in. People who practice their art don't just do a job, they own it and live it. They enjoy the beauty of the work itself and the contribution that they make.

Your art is meaningful work that puts you into a state of flow, where you are so swallowed up by your passion for what you are doing that you become focused beyond all reason on the task, the activity, or the work. It's what American psychologist Abraham Maslow refers to as "self-actualization," when a person goes beyond taking care of their basic needs and creates something that gives them a sense of fulfillment. Your art allows you to reclaim your creative spirit as well as your enthusiasm and imagination, and it will satisfy you more than other work or leisure activities ever can.

At our seminars I've had the pleasure of hearing the stories of many kinds of people who have found their art. They are the retirees with the big smiles on their faces who get so excited when they tell me how they found/created work that they can play at. What I've learned from listening to

> Art enables us to find ourselves and lose ourselves at the same time.
>
> —Thomas Merton

these folks is that your art can be found in anything. For example, I've heard stories from a former car mechanic who found his art in restoring and selling old cars; a retired plumber who ended up working happily at Home Depot; people who create websites and teach boomers to become computer savvy; and people who grow beautiful gardens and regularly win the annual best garden award. They are all practicing their art, pursuing their passion, creating something, or offering services to help others; their art makes them feel really good about themselves and what they are doing.

People who follow their dreams and practice their art—work that lights them up—are the happiest retirees I've met because they live the most satisfying and fulfilling retirements. Being able to say "I built this table," or "I created this blog," or "I helped this person," is much more satisfying than just saying you are retired, like many people do. Find your art and you will enjoy a great retirement. When you connect purpose to passion, you can't lose.

Another Retirement Lesson from Japan

You'll recall from earlier in the book the idea of *ikigai*, which is the Japanese word for one's purpose. *Shokunin* is another interesting Japanese concept, meaning "mastery of one's profession or art." It's based on helping others by delivering a product or service of the highest quality to one's community. By extension, *shokunin kishitsu* means "craftsman's spirit." The Japanese believe that there is pride in every profession, as long as you do it to the best of your ability. Cooks, garbage collectors, restaurant servers, plumbers, teachers, and office workers are all highly respected in Japanese culture because of their *shokunin kishitsu*. If you want a great example of Japanese *shokunin*, google *Jiro Dreams of Sushi*, a movie about the first-ever three-star Michelin sushi chef, who worked well into his nineties trying to perfect what he loved to do.

Finding your *shokunin kishitsu* will take your retirement to a whole new level. Working at always trying to become better at whatever type of work you choose to do—or, in fact, at any activity you engage in—is something that will unlock the potential within you. The pursuit of perfection is a constant challenge and something you can enjoy doing for a long time. Two sources of *shokunin kishitsu* for me are my blog writing and doing retirement presentations. I plan on working hard to upgrade the quality of my writing and presentation skills, and that should keep me happily busy for many years. Find your art, practice *shokunin kishitsu*, and you will be one of the happiest retirees around.

How to Find/Create Great Work

Everyone has a special purpose, a special talent or gift to give to others, and it is your duty to discover what it is. Your special talent is God's gift to you. What you do with your talent is your gift to God.

—*Gautama Chopra*

We wrote about the concept of *ikigai* in our first book, *Victory Lap Retirement*, and in Chapter 9 of this book. Here, we will use that concept to help us find/create work for ourselves that has a lot of purpose and meaning attached to it. It's a simple process that is dependent upon you using your imagination in combination with recognizing your strengths and weaknesses; knowing what you are passionate about; and understanding what things you could monetize and make some extra income doing.

Copy the diagram on the next page into your journal and then write out as many answers as you can to the four questions that follow. Take your time, do some soul-searching, and see what comes to you.

1. What do you love to do?
   • What activities get you excited and make you feel good?
   • What activities do you have a passion for?
   • What activities put you in a state of flow?
   • What would you do for free if you didn't need the money?

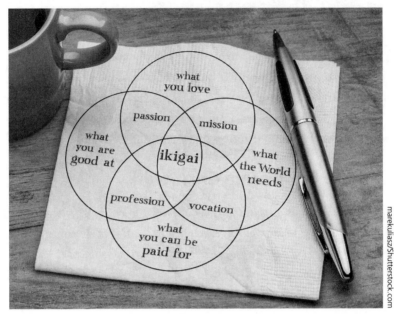

marekuliasz/Shutterstock.com

2. What are you good at?
- What skills, talents, and abilities do you have?
- What things come easily to you?
- What do you do better than anyone else?

3. What do people need?
- What problems do people have that you can help solve?
- How can you help improve/change the lives of others?
- What can you do to make people happy?

4. What could you do and be paid for?
- Which passions/skills/hobbies can you monetize?
- What value can you create for others?
- Do people need what you are offering?
- Will people pay for what you are offering?

After you come up with your answers, start testing them so you can weed out the weaker ones. Show what you have come up with to others for their input and guidance, and have someone with experience review your plan and test it for soundness.

This simple diagram worked for me, and it can work for you. If you take your time and really focus, you will be amazed with the answers that you come up with. Figure out the best option for you and then go after it with all you've got. The payoff is huge in terms of being able to create a life that you don't have to retire from, one where you are your own boss, making money doing stuff you really love to do and where you have the flexibility and the means to enjoy the leisure time you want. Believe me, retirement doesn't get much more heavenly than that.

The Story of Jack

I always tell this story about Jack at our seminars, as it is a great example of someone who used the *ikigai* diagram to create a wonderful Victory Lap for himself. I always smile when I tell it, because Jack is just like me. We come from the same career background, and it's nice to tell a story with a happy ending.

Jack is a good guy who was packaged off from his thirty-six–year corporate banking job and was suffering from a bad case of retirement shock. His wife hated to see how he was struggling and asked if I could have a talk with him to see if I could help get him back on track. After the usual re-telling of banking stories and the accompanying laughter (this is what ex-bankers do), it came out in the conversation that Jack after a bad day would decompress after dinner by going down to the basement and working on renovating it. I guess hitting things with a hammer made him feel good, and it was far better than sitting down on the couch having a few beers and watching TV, like I did.

I asked him to show me his basement, and it was just beautiful. It was quite obvious that Jack was good with his hands and knew what he was doing. After talking further, it came out that he had even built his cottage with his father. They built the whole thing by themselves, doing all the plumbing, electrical, woodwork, and even the pouring of cement for the foundation. Upon hearing this, I suggested Jack fill out an *ikigai* diagram, and it was easy to figure out a good possibility for him: doing cottage renovations.

At first, Jack pushed back because of the fear of starting his own business, and he came up with a list of excuses. He had never run his own business before and he didn't know how he would be able to get customers. Being a cottage owner myself, I told him that getting customers would be easy. Getting good tradespeople who show up when they are supposed to and do quality work on budget is as rare as winning the lottery. Cottagers talk, and I told Jack that if he did one job that was good, the word would spread and he would be up to his ears in work in no time.

Jack pondered things over for a while and eventually took the plunge, and before long, people were lining up to have him repair things for them. This led to another problem, though, as Jack's wife got a little mad over him working so much. The three of us had another meeting where a compromise was struck: Jack would only work weekdays from eight to four and never on the weekends, which were reserved for family who visited the cottage regularly in the summer. There was no working in the winter, and instead Jack and his wife would winter in Costa Rica and have the kids come down and visit.

It was a win-win for everyone, but Jack and his wife decided to take it one step further. They decided to sell their home in Toronto and use part of the proceeds to help their daughter buy a bigger house in a better area with a downstairs walkout. Jack fixed up the basement, and that is where they hang their hat when they are in town; when they're not there, their grandkids use the basement as a play area—another great win-win. And even better, Jack used the money left over to boost his retirement savings and help save for the grandkids' education. Now that is what I call a smiling Jack!

I hear a lot of these kinds of success stories from people at our retirement seminars, and I could tell many more about people reinventing themselves and launching new careers on their own terms and in any number of creative ways.

Great Work Doesn't Have to Be Paid Work

Some of us will not have a need or even a desire in retirement to make more money but will still want to find a source of great work for ourselves. If so, we can still use the *ikigai* diagram to help us. All we have to do is ignore the section on "What kind of work could you do and be paid for?"

Let's use Jack the cottage renovator as an example. If he didn't need the money, he could have been inspired by former President Jimmy Carter and volunteered at Habitat for Humanity building houses for the needy. That charitable work would put Jack's skills to good use helping others, and he would be happy doing work that he loves to do. There is nothing more satisfying in retirement than helping others who are less well-off than you by doing work that's interesting, challenging, and gratifying—where you can see the payoff from your own efforts.

Summary

Working in some way is a key component of a vibrant and satisfying retirement. You may want to work for only a few years once you've left your full-time career behind, but there is no better way to keep you healthy, make you feel good about yourself, and protect you from becoming bored. The key is to avoid bad work and find good work, or even better—great work.

My Story

While I don't have a lot of money, I have enough financial assets to retire, sit back on the couch, and watch the world go by. But I can't do that because it would be a form of Retirement Hell for me. I know myself well enough to know that I need to be working in retirement if I want to be happy, and that's why I plan on working for as long as I can. Working gives me pride and a sense of meaning, and I would lose my mind sitting around doing nothing all day. Leisure activities alone cannot replace the type of fulfillment I get from paid work.

One of my biggest mistakes after getting pushed out of my banking job was not taking some time off to regroup before starting something else. I instinctively went into survival mode and found a new job within a couple days of leaving. Instead of taking my time and finding good (or great) work that I would enjoy, I defaulted to doing what I was comfortable with (banking), which was a bad move because I had grown to dislike my former job for a number of reasons. And yet there I was, in basically the same place that I needed to get away from, which was kind of dumb. Please learn from my mistakes.

I just couldn't work in a corporate setting anymore. I was tired of the office politics and the need to toe the line. I needed to escape and be me. I needed to do work that I liked, in my own way, and reap the rewards of my own efforts. To find this new work, I started to go through the process of finding my *ikigai*, and during a bout of early morning writing it came to me that I should write a book about retirement. Because of all the struggles I experienced trying to figure this retirement thing out for myself, I felt people could save time and avoid a lot of stress learning from what I went through. That book became *Victory Lap Retirement*, and a whole new career was born.

Following is what I discovered about myself while going through the *ikigai* process:

- My former job equipped me with marketing, investing, and coaching skills that I could use in my new business.
- I could generate active income through book sales, conducting seminars, and retirement coaching.
- Based on my own personal struggles with retirement, I knew that many retirees could benefit from what I had to offer.

I knew I was on the right track in writing the book, as I couldn't wait to get up in the mornings and start writing. I also really enjoy giving seminars and hearing about other people's retirement stories. Over the years, I've had the privilege of meeting many retirees who have managed to start businesses aligned with their passion. They are the ones with a big smile on their faces, with a twinkle in their eyes. Their fear is gone, having been replaced with a lot of happiness, thanks to what they are doing in Victory Lap.

I take great pride in the fact that I can help others save time and avoid much confusion and frustration by offering them a caring outside perspective on their situation and helping them reach their full retirement potential and live more fulfilling, happier lives. I show them what they are capable of and help take their fear away, and doing this brings me great joy. I found the great work that I always wanted—I found my art—all because of a simple chart!

My work is great work to me because it satisfies most of my needs and values. It gives me the autonomy that I need, and boy, does it ever feel good to be able to call the shots after all those years of taking orders from someone else. I know in order to be happy, I need to contribute, to feel a sense of achievement, to feel valued, and to be recognized, and my work delivers that to me in spades. I realize now that it was God's plan for me to be a teacher and help people connect to their own purposeful missions. I view my speaking and writing as my creative expression; it's my "art," and I use my art to help alleviate retirement pain for boomers. I love it when, after I've given a presentation, people are excited and smiling and thanking me for my efforts. That's a big deal for me, and it makes me feel really good inside knowing that I have helped someone. Bottom line: my work fulfills me, and Victory Lap doesn't get much better than that.

Questions for Self-Reflection
- What type of work excites you?
- What type of work makes you lose track of time?
- What are you very good at?
- What do you want to become very good at?
- What type of work would you do if you won the lottery?
- To what extent does the work you are considering match your natural abilities and support your key values?
- Is the work **work**, or is it play to you? Do you love it so much that it is your art?
- How many hours a week do you plan to work in your Victory Lap?
- Are you doing the work that you really need to do?
- Does your work make you happy and feel good, or does it just make you more money?
- If you want to run your own business, what excites you the most about that prospect?

Simple Truths
- Working part-time in Victory Lap will give you the time, flexibility, and cash flow to do the things you couldn't do before or couldn't otherwise afford.
- A person's decision to work or not and what type of work they decide to do will have a significant impact on their happiness levels.

- Work can be a wonderful form of escape from too much togetherness as a retired couple.
- Working forces you to keep mentally and physically active; it keeps you engaged with the world and up to speed with all the changes coming at you.
- You may be more prepared than you realize to find/create new work because of the valuable skills you developed over the years.
- You are more capable than you think.
- Anyone can find a job if they really want to.
- Retirement is too short to be stuck doing work you hate.
- Starting a new business will take more time and money than you think.
- One of the biggest regrets you can have in retirement is not doing what you dreamed of doing but didn't have the guts to do.
- Great work is work that nourishes the spirit as well as pays the bills.
- Work is not work unless you would rather be doing something else.
- When we are able to connect "who we are" with "what we do," retirement is pretty good.

PART 4

CREATE A HEAVENLY RETIREMENT FOR YOURSELF

16

Time to Become a Retirement Rebel

Here's to the crazy ones. The misfits. The rebels. The troublemakers.
The round pegs in the square holes. The ones who see things differently
. . . because the people who are crazy enough to think they can change
the world are the ones who do.
　　—Steve Jobs

The boomers I love to hang around with are bad-ass people in their sixties, seventies, and eighties who have ripped up the old retirement rule book on aging and retirement. They are ordinary people who are doing extraordinary things and, in fact, they are anything but retired. I fondly refer to them as Retirement Rebels (also known as Victory Lappers), as they refuse to follow the old-fashioned beliefs about "old people" and traditional retirement.

They are the trailblazers who have regained the curiosity and wonder of a child, traveling the world to see and experience new places, entering marathons in different cities, learning to use new technology, volunteering, starting new businesses, and posting all about it on social media. They love their freedom and view the world as their retirement playground. Retirement Rebels like to play a lot. They still have plenty of gas left in the tank, and they want more—much more—out of their remaining years. They know it's their turn and that they have the freedom to do retirement differently, not the traditional way society says it should be lived. You can learn a lot from watching Retirement Rebels in action.

The challenge with becoming a Retirement Rebel is that there are not a lot of recognized role models out there you can follow. The advertisers used to have a good one—the guy the beer commercials touted as the world's most interesting man, "A person who sees the fun in life and lives each day to the fullest. He's humorous and outrageous but never boring. His only regret is not knowing what regret feels like." I love that tag line, and he would have been a good role model for people in their Victory Lap, but unfortunately, the company decided to retire *him*.

LESSONS FROM A PANDEMIC

Dr. Anthony Fauci is a great Retirement Rebel role model. At age seventy-nine, he was America's top public health expert during the COVID-19 crisis, and that's not all. He maintains his high energy levels by watching what he eats and fitting in a three-mile run every day to keep healthy and reduce stress. All I can say is that I like his style and would love to be in his kind of shape when I turn seventy-nine.

Fauci is a straight shooter and tells it like it is. Due to his blunt assessment of the pandemic, he received death threats that resulted in the need for a security detail. Nonetheless, he doesn't work for the money; he works because contributing to his country and saving lives gives him purpose and makes him feel good inside. Why would he ever retire from something he loves to do?

A true Retirement Rebel if I ever saw one!

The Top Ten Characteristics of Retirement Rebels

To help guide you into becoming your own version of a Retirement Rebel, I have put together a list of the ten most common characteristics shared by the Retirement Rebels I have had the pleasure of meeting and hanging around with.

1. They Live Their Values

Retirement Rebels are authentic; they live their values and don't pretend to be someone they aren't. They know themselves well: what makes them happy, what frustrates them, and what makes them sad. They are fully transparent—what you see is what you get. They are comfortable with themselves just the way they are. They live and breathe the retirement principles and are smart about what they eat, the work that they do, and how they spend their time. They're straightforward and honest and aren't afraid to voice their opinions and tell it like it is if they think something is wrong. They have little patience for putting up with a lot of nonsense; they don't have time for that anymore.

2. They Are Proud but Not Too Proud to Listen and Learn

Retirement Rebels don't like to conform; they like to do things their own way. They earn what they get and don't expect anyone to do them any favors. They know that they alone are responsible for their retirement successes or failures. However, they are willing to listen and accept feedback, both negative and positive, so that they can learn and have the most fulfilling Victory Lap possible.

3. They Have a Positive Attitude

Retirement Rebels are optimistic about the future because they are in charge of it and know exactly what they want to do, where they want to go, and most importantly "why." They have a high degree of self-confidence and are less stressed than other retirees because they understand their financial position and know that no matter what happens they will be OK. They know they will always be able to get a job if they really need or want one, and that they can always learn new things. They know they don't need much in terms of material possessions in order to be happy. They realize that millions of people have much less than they do but still manage to lead happy lives.

Retirement Rebels are egoless and, because they are egoless, they don't compare themselves with others or worry about being "liked" on social media, because they don't care about what others think. They know at this stage of their lives that they don't have to waste time and energy trying to impress anyone or worry about being accepted anymore. They compete only with themselves, chasing after their own personal goals. They don't crave the spotlight or need the applause—they do what they want to do and what needs to be done, regardless of whether anyone is watching or not. They never stop believing in themselves and what they are capable of, but they are also willing to be vulnerable and show emotion. They understand the importance of telling someone they love them while they still can. They like to laugh a lot, especially at themselves.

4. They Have No Retirement Excuses

Some Retirement Rebels might not have the benefit of a lot of money or maybe, like me, they got pushed out early from the only job they ever had, but they don't let that stop them from enjoying a great Victory Lap. They are willing to do the things that less successful retirees aren't willing to do. They control their own destiny rather than letting fate and others decide the future for them. They believe that choice more than chance determines the quality of their retirement.

They don't feel sorry for themselves and never feel they are a helpless victim of circumstance. If there's a problem, they solve it. For example, if they can't meet their friends for coffee anymore because they can't drive, they learn to use Uber. And if they can't hear so well anymore, they are not embarrassed to get some of those fancy hearing aids to fix the problem. They choose not to let stubbornness or pride prevent them from enjoying a great retirement.

> It's not about the cards you're dealt, but how you play the hand.
> —Randy Pausch

5. They View Retirement Differently Than Most Retirees

Retirement Rebels are really no different than you, they just look at retirement differently and do things that most retirees don't. They refuse to be held back by outdated myths about aging, and they laugh at those outdated commercials about retirees on TV because they know that real retirement is nothing like that.

They refuse to let chronological age constrain and limit their perspective on what is possible for them in retirement. They don't trust the system to take care of them, so they figure out ways to take care of themselves. They take full control because it's their problem and they will find their own solution. They don't waste time blaming others for their problems.

> We do not stop playing because we get old; we grow old because we stop playing.
> — George Bernard Shaw

6. They Have a Growth Mind-set

Retirement Rebels have a strong inner voice that is constantly telling them to never be satisfied—to keep stretching, exploring,

learning, and experiencing. They are the retirees that have created a bucket list a mile long and plan on knocking things off that
list as long as they can.

> Every moment of one's
> existence, one is growing
> into more or retreating
> into less. One is always
> living a little more or
> dying a little bit.
>
> —Norman Mailer

Retirement Rebels have a beginner's mind-set and know it's
growth that generates happiness,
not retiring (as in withdrawing
from the world) before your time.
They are growth-oriented retirees,
which Abraham Maslow refers to as
"self-actualizers." They have a need
for continual personal growth, always working on "becoming"
what they are capable of. They don't want to leave anything on
the table; they want to be fully used up when their time comes.
They want to know that they took enough risks, played hard
enough, dreamed big enough, and went after their dreams with
everything they had.

Some Retirement Rebels feel the need to go even further,
pursuing goals beyond the self by finding a cause, a need, or a
problem to be solved and devoting their efforts to that. They
get their deepest satisfaction and feeling that they mattered by
using their gifts to make a difference in others' lives. And some
Retirement Rebels, like me, feel the need to do both.

Retirement Rebels invest their time and energy developing
new skills, solving new problems, acquiring new knowledge,
and figuring out ways to make their retirement even better.
They are curious and are always on the improve, updating
skills and taking online courses on things they want to learn
more about.

When they physically can't do those things anymore, they
know it will be time to officially retire.

7. They Aren't Scared to Fail

Retirement Rebels never allow fear and uncertainty to block them from trying something new. They ignore their fears and keep pushing forward.

They are successful in Victory Lap because they think about challenges and failure differently. They know failure is just another way to learn and grow, so they look forward to failing a lot. They are not afraid of being judged, nor are they afraid of looking foolish or stupid. They know that living outside their comfort zone is what makes retirement exciting. They like to live on the edge, and they are willing to take some chances just because they can, knowing they have nothing to lose. This new stage of their lives gives them freedom they never had before.

> The only mistake is not to risk making one.
> —Max Lucado

8. They Are Careful About Who They Hang Out With

Retirement Rebels are very selective about how they spend their time and with whom they spend it. They avoid people with bad attitudes and bad habits they're trying to stay away from. They don't like to hang around boring old farts: retirees who think and act old, do boring things, go to the same old places, hang out with the same people, watch the same boring crap on TV, and complain about the same boring things day after day. They steer clear of retirees who whine about their inability to get a part-time job, whine about their former employer, and whine about how the government is always screwing them. They are worried that if they hang around the boring whiners, some of that negativity might rub off on them, and the thought of that scares them.

Instead, Retirement Rebels like to hang around other rebels and talk about how exciting retirement is and all the possibilities; people who will share with them their dreams and aspirations and give them some new ideas about what they should try next. They are picky about what tribes they join. They like belonging to tribes that include young people because younger people challenge them and influence them to act and think young.

9. They Love Simplicity

Retirement Rebels strip down their lives to the bare essentials, the few things they really enjoy; avoiding unnecessary maintenance by getting rid of big homes they no longer need, for example. They know they don't need a big car, expensive jewelry, designer clothes, or a big eighty-inch TV to be happy or to convince others how successful they are. They feel comfortable wearing whatever they want because they don't care how they look to others. They know that it is the person who is wearing the clothes that really matters.

10. They Love to Break the Rules

Retirement Rebels don't like to be told what to do. If they want to climb a mountain or volunteer to build a school in Africa or become a stand-up comedian, they do it. They don't allow anyone or anything to hold them back from what they want to do. They enjoy breaking rules and traditions just because they can. They hate to hear people tell them what they can't do. When someone tells them they are not good enough to start their own business, they create one. They love to defy people's expectations and prove them wrong. They feel compelled to prove what they are capable of and what is possible if a person wants it badly enough. They will never allow the opinions of others keep them from chasing their dreams. They like to challenge the status quo and push against long-held beliefs about how they should act and live in retirement. They are determined and like to take control to shape their own destiny. They want to create their own version of Retirement Heaven instead of just accepting what comes their way.

> *Life should not be a journey to the grave with the intention of arriving safely in a pretty and well preserved body, but rather to skid in broadside in a cloud of smoke, thoroughly used up, totally worn out, and loudly proclaiming "Wow! What a ride!"*
>
> —Hunter S. Thompson

Summary

My hope is that after reading this chapter you will refuse to accept the old retirement stereotypes and instead join our tribe and become a Retirement Rebel. Don't settle for a mediocre retirement when you are capable of so much more. Stop acting your age, whatever that is supposed to mean, and go do your thing,

> Life is like a bicycle. You don't fall off unless you stop pedaling.
>
> —Claude Pepper

because it's your turn and you don't want to waste it by not taking risks and by playing small.

My Story

The first Retirement Rebel I ever had the pleasure of meeting was Ernie Zelinski, and his book *How to Retire Happy, Wild, and Free* was one of the resources that saved me from Retirement Hell and put me on the path I'm currently on. Ernie thinks differently than most retirees and likes to joke around a lot, and we have become good friends.

Today when I look at myself in the mirror, I don't see an old retired man looking back at me. What I see is a Retirement Rebel with a mischievous grin on his face who feels and acts twenty years younger than I actually am. I'm not concerned about making a lot of money, because my self-worth is no longer tied to my net worth. I don't care how much others have or what I don't have, and it feels so good to be able to say that. I don't need to prove myself to anyone because I don't care about that stuff anymore.

I enjoy being a Retirement Rebel because I can free my inner John Wayne. I don't feel the need to conform anymore. I did that most of my life while working, and I'm not willing to take any more orders. I now decide what constitutes a success to me, and I just do my thing. I know I can't please everyone, and I'm OK with that. I just want to be the authentic version of me and succeed or fail on my own terms. I'm going to do it my way from now on. I choose where I want to live, what I want to do, and who I want to hang around with. I used to dye my hair to hide the gray but have decided not to do that anymore.

I like hanging around other Retirement Rebels because they remind me not to buy into the bullshit we're told about turning sixty-five and what we can and can't do. The truth is, a person's age doesn't mean anything. I swim with a Retirement Rebel who plans on celebrating his eightieth birthday by attempting Ironman Florida, and his wife celebrated her own eightieth birthday recently by completing a 2,000-meter swim. Now that is a couple the advertisers should make a retirement commercial about!

The truth is that you're never too old if your heart is willing. I turned sixty-five on October 15, 2019. Most men my age are retired and spend a lot of time watching sports on TV, but that's just not me. I would rather participate instead of watching, and I refuse to give in to the couch and the remote. I want my life to mean something. I don't want to settle. I plan on continuing to challenge myself and always be on the outlook for another mountain to climb until I can't climb anymore, because I love the way it makes me feel.

A true retirement rebel, Pat was always looking for another mountain to climb.

I'm planning on signing up for my own Ironman Triathlon in 2022 just because I can. The thought of attempting an event that less than 1 percent of people in the world finish appeals to me. It makes me proud to be referred to as a Retirement Rebel. It just sounds so much sexier than retiree, don't you think?

Questions for Self-Reflection

- Are you a Retirement Rebel?
- Do you want to be?
- Who are your Retirement Rebel role models?
- What qualities do they display that you find attractive?
- How can you make a positive contribution to the world around you?
- Are you taking enough risks and chasing after your dreams so that you can become the best you can be?

Simple Truths

- Becoming a Retirement Rebel isn't easy, but it's worth it.
- Retirement Rebels refuse to be conned into acting old and retiring before their time.
- Many Retirement Rebels have little in the way of money, but they are some of the most upbeat and happy people I have met.
- Retirement Rebels know that any day they learn a new lesson is a great day.
- Retirement Rebels know that they will never regret the risks they took, only the ones they didn't take.
- Retirement Rebels live like there is no tomorrow because there might not be.
- Retirement Rebels know that generosity through helping others makes them feel good and gives them a strong sense of gratitude.
- Retirement Rebels know that comfort and leisure are great, but they are not enough in order to be happy.
- Retirement Rebels know that merely surviving is not living. They know they need to grow in order to thrive.
- Retirement Rebels speak the truth about what they see, and they own what they say.
- Retirement Rebels know that they are capable of far more than they have done so far.
- We're all going to die, but why go quietly?

17

Retirement Lifestyle Design

Creating a Good Ending
to Your Movie

*Although no one can go back and make a brand new start, anyone can
start from now and make a brand new ending.*
  —*Lori Bard*

If you have done a lot of self-reflection and answered the end-of-chapter questions throughout the book honestly, by this point you will have learned a lot about yourself, both good and bad. You should have a sense of how you are wired, what your needs and values are, what your fears and challenges are, and what your new purpose is. This level of awareness is something that most retirees lack, so consider yourself ahead of the game.

We are going to take everything you have learned and use it to design a retirement lifestyle using the nine retirement principles as the foundation, but before we can do that, you need to create a retirement vision for yourself. Because without knowing exactly what you want your retirement to look and feel like, you're going to have a hard time getting there. You will get frustrated and give up. You will default to following the traditional retirement status quo and end up doing what everyone else is doing. You might, for example, take up golf or tennis because that's what your retired friends are doing. You might decide to move somewhere warmer or downsize because you've seen on TV that's what retirees like you are doing. You might decide to go on cruises because a lot of retirees are going on cruises. Doing these things can be great if that's what you really want. But if you're just following the pack and automatically doing what everyone else is doing, odds are you're going to end up having a lousy retirement.

You need to figure out for yourself your own mission and your own vision of Retirement Heaven. Close your eyes and imagine what a great retirement looks and feels like to you.

- Where are you living?
- What do you look like?
- What adventures are you going on?
- Are you working? At what? And to what extent?
- Are you surrounded with a loving family and friends?

The clearer you visualize retirement success (whatever that looks like to you) and the more detailed the mental picture you create in your mind, the quicker and easier you will get there. You want to create a retirement vision so compelling and exciting that it pulls you out of bed in the morning, motivating and driving you toward the future that you want.

To get the required clarity, you need to answer three key questions:

- Who are you?
- Who do you want to be?
- What do you want to do?

Who Are You?

If you have answered all the questions for self-reflection honestly, it should be easy for you to answer this big question. And if you're not completely thrilled with the answers you've turned up, don't despair—there is still time to create a better, healthier, happier you.

A movie that resonates strongly with me is *A Christmas Carol*, based on the Charles Dickens novel by the same name. Each year, it reminds me that we all have the power to change the outcome of our future, just like Ebenezer Scrooge did. In the movie, the Ghost of Christmas Yet to Come shows Scrooge what his future will look like if he continues on the same path. Scrooge comes to understand that the future he is shown is alterable and that he alone has the power to change his fate before it is too late.

Just like Scrooge did, you have been doing a lot of self-reflection as you have progressed through this book. Perhaps there were some thoughts that concerned you; maybe you're scared that you are on the fast track to Retirement Hell. If so, don't worry, because things don't have to turn out that way. Like Scrooge, we can't change what's happened in the past, but we can learn from it and influence the future and live much better than we have been living by making good choices from this day forward. You still have time to fix things, but you have to hurry.

Questions for Self-Reflection
- Pretend you are the character Scrooge. You are meeting the ghost from the future and you're being shown your own funeral. What are people saying about you?
- Do you like what they are saying about you?
- How do you want to be remembered?

Who Do You Want to Be?

To answer this second big question, you need to go back to the movie of your life and, like Scrooge, ask yourself this: What would you *like* people to say about you at your funeral?

Rather than, "He wasn't a very good father or a good husband. He was always stressed out, never seemed happy, was always complaining about his job, and would spend most of his time after work sitting on the couch watching TV, eating chips and drinking beer," wouldn't you prefer some of the following examples?

- "He was a great father, a generous friend, and one of the happiest people I ever met."
- "He didn't really care about money and spent what he earned in Victory Lap Retirement on amazing experiences with his family."
- "He had a sense of adventure and loved being known as a Retirement Rebel. He wasn't afraid to try new things and stretch himself. I don't think he ever really retired. He was always learning and doing stuff. He loved helping people."

Another way to think of this exercise is to consider who you want to be in terms of creating a new LinkedIn profile for yourself online. You're starting from scratch, in essence doing a complete reconstruction of who you are. Think about both who you want to be, and who you don't want to be—those qualities about yourself that you really don't like and that you'll need to work on. You need to decide on what parts of you that you want to keep, what parts you want to add, and what parts of you that you need to throw away.

Questions for Self-Reflection
- What do you like about yourself?
- What don't you like about yourself?
- What do you need to change?

Changing Habits Is Hard, but Possible If You Want It Badly Enough

There's a difference between interest and commitment. When you're interested in doing something, you do it only when it's convenient. When you're committed to something, you accept no excuses; only results.

—Ken Blanchard

Your retirement vision will not happen until you eliminate the things that have been holding you back—your bad destructive habits. Maybe you eat too much, drink too much, shop too much, watch too much TV, spend too much time on social media, or get high every night just to get yourself through another day. In order to achieve the retirement outcome you want, you must take a stand and refuse to live like that anymore, so you can become the person you want to be and live the life you want in Victory Lap. It's time to stop doing all that stuff you know you shouldn't be doing. The stuff you don't like about yourself, the things that you are in conflict with, the things that keep you stuck. Changing habits that have been a part of you for a long time is hard work. But is it worth it? Damn right it is!

Mike would always get a headache when they argued like that.

Willpower Alone Will Not Be Enough

I know habit change is hard because as I write this, I'm trying to change some of my own bad habits. I'm not embarrassed to admit that I tried making these habit changes before, back when I was working full-time, but I failed because I wasn't "all in." I tried to rely solely on willpower, but I learned that willpower by itself isn't enough to make lasting change happen.

Using willpower requires a great deal of effort and energy because when you are not fully committed to something, there is a constant internal conflict going on inside you. You are pushing yourself to do something that you know is good for you, but when your heart really isn't in it, you will probably end up failing like I did.

To succeed in becoming the person you want to be, you need to have a strong "why" for making the change. Ask yourself why it is so important for you to make changes. There could be many reasons.

- Maybe it's because you love your family and you want to maximize the time you can spend with them on this planet.
- Maybe it's because you want to have enough energy to play with your grandkids and be around for their graduation.
- Maybe it's because you want to walk up a flight of stairs without being winded and feeling like you are going to have a heart attack.
- Maybe your relationship with your spouse and kids sucks and you want to fix things.
- Maybe you're bored out of your mind from sitting on the couch watching TV for most of the day and you need to find something fulfilling to do, like finding meaningful work or starting your own business, before you lose your mind.
- Maybe it's because you want to avoid going to a nursing home.

Instead of relying on willpower to force yourself to do something, use your "why," your core purpose, as the driving force—the reason to do something so you can reap the benefits. It's sort of like flipping a switch so you don't feel like you're forcing or depriving yourself; rather, you're driven by your mission and a positive growth mind-set.

When you have a strong enough "why," you can break through the bad habits that are holding you back. You'll not be tempted to skip your gym workout, eat that big bag of BBQ chips, drink another beer, or give up on that new business you just started. You'll stay on track, show up, and do the work because you know exactly what the payoff will be, and you want that payoff bad. When you have a strong enough "why," you will do whatever it is you need to do to reach your goal. I guarantee if one of your kids needed some medicine to survive and you didn't have the money to pay for it, you would be able to find a job to get the money. It's all about the size of your "why."

> With a strong enough "why" you can overcome any "how."
> —Tony Robbins

Bottom line: if you don't have a strong "why" and you rely only on willpower, chances are you will end up getting what you have always gotten. But willpower and a strong "why" together are very powerful in creating new, good habits. And once the new behavior is firmly in place, you will no longer have to use willpower anymore. For instance, to help me lose weight I have made it a habit not to eat dessert. Now that it is a habit, it's automatic, I don't think about it, and I no longer have to struggle with that decision every time I go out for dinner.

Something to be aware of is that you need to be careful about the people you hang out with when you are trying to break old habits and create new ones. A study at Harvard Business School found that people who hang out with smokers are more likely to smoke; people who hang out with obese people are more likely to gain weight; and people who hang out with positive, happy, and successful people are more likely to become positive, happy, and successful. Makes perfect sense to me, and that's why I'm choosy about who I hang out with. But

> You are the average of the five people you spend the most time with.
>
> —Jim Rohn

it doesn't stop there, because you also need to be careful of the environment in which you spend your time.

To help with habit change, you need to create an environment for yourself where discipline and willpower aren't even required, by removing any possible temptation. For instance, if you are trying to lose weight, throw out all the stuff that you need to avoid eating, like the processed meats in the fridge and, again, that big bag of BBQ chips in the cupboard. (Can you tell what my weakness is when it comes to snacks?) If you want to cut down on drinking, get rid of the beer in the fridge and your favorite booze in the liquor cabinet, and stay away from places where you usually "have a few" for a while, until your new habit kicks in. And when it does kick in, retirement becomes so much simpler because we know what we want and what to do without having to think about it. The daily decision about whether you should go to the gym or sit on the couch with a beer and watch Netflix is eliminated, and this can help you avoid a lot of stress.

Questions for Self-Reflection
- What destructive behavior, coping mechanisms (drinking, self-medicating, poor eating habits, etc.) are getting in the way of where you want to go?
- If you could change one bad habit in your life, what would it be?
- What would be the payoff for getting rid of that bad habit?
- Which one of your habits would you not like to see your children adopt?

- Which bad habits do your friends share with you?
- What negative environments do you need to avoid?
- What makes you feel the most negative about yourself?
- Do you follow the advice you give others?
- What aspects of yourself do you hide from others?
- Do you keep making promises to yourself that you don't keep?
- What negative things do you see in others that you see in yourself as well?
- Do you have a strong enough "why" to stop living the life you have been living and to start living the life you want?

What Do You Want to Do?

If you are bored with life, if you don't get up every morning with a burning desire to do things—you don't have enough goals.

—*Lou Holtz*

Now we come to the third of the big questions you need to ask yourself: What is it you want to do? To answer this, you need to think about what outcomes you want, what you want to achieve, and how you are going to achieve those things. Following the five steps below will help you to put specific goals in place that align with your vision to get you to where you want to be in retirement, doing what you want to do.

Step 1: Defining Your Lifestyle Goals

The first step involves setting some big-picture goals and creating a vision statement for each of the retirement principles that are your biggest concerns, the ones that are causing you the most stress.

Obstacles are those frightful things you see when you take your eyes off your goal.

—Henry Ford

Following are some examples of some of my own big-picture goals:

- **My social goal (Retirement Principle #1):** I don't want to be alone. I want to love and feel loved. I want to be a good father and husband, to have lots of good friendships, and to contribute in some meaningful way to the world.

- **My health goal (Retirement Principle #2):** I don't want to lose my health and not be able to do the things that I want to do. I want to lose weight so I will be able to walk a lot while on vacation without running out of breath. I want to look good in the mirror after getting out of the shower and not scare myself. I want to see my abs one last time before I die.

- **My travel/adventure goal (Retirement Principle #5):** I want to travel the world and learn about people and their cultures. I want to learn and experience different things.

- **My work goal (Retirement Principle #9):** I want to teach investment advisors and financial planners how they can help their clients achieve retirement success. Most people (the growth-oriented ones) will struggle with retirement transition like I did. Trusted advisors can help their clients avoid a lot of stress by educating them about what they are about to go through and what they need to do to achieve optimum retirement well-being.

Step 2: Setting Objectives

For each big-vision goal, you need to establish some smaller goals—specific objectives that will help you to achieve your desired outcomes. It's important to ensure that the objectives you set are realistic, are measurable, and ideally, have a specific time frame attached to them. Not all goals need a specific time frame attached, as they could be more general, but most do.

Using my big-picture health goal as an example, following are the actions I have decided I need to take to accomplish it:

- I want to get back to under two hundred pounds and fit into my size 36 pants by April 30, 2021.
- I want to be working out a minimum of two hours a day, six days a week by July 31, 2021.
- I want to attempt Ironman Cozumel on November 21, 2022.

Or, using my vision for travel and adventure as an example, I'm planning a trip with a friend to the Bahamas in March 2021 (COVID-19 pandemic permitting) so I can learn to scuba dive and get certified. Learning a new skill like this will open up a whole new world with lots of new adventures for me. My travel and adventure goal is a good one, as it positively impacts a number of the other retirement principles: my relationship with a friend will be strengthened, I'll be learning something new that will challenge my brain, and I will also be getting some good physical exercise out of it as well.

The more specific you can be in setting goals and objectives, the easier it will be to see your vision in your mind, to measure your progress toward each objective, and to accomplish it. The goals you choose can be very challenging, such as climbing Mount Kilimanjaro, or quite simple, like saving $100 a month to go on a special fishing trip next year.

Goals are dreams with deadlines.

—Diana Scharf Hunt

As discussed earlier, make sure you have a strong "why" for setting each of your goals. Your "why" will supply the intrinsic motivation you will need in order to turn them into a reality. Think about how you will feel after hitting each goal. Think about the smile you will have on your face when you try on the new medium-sized golf shirt instead of the XL, or was it an XXL? Visualize how you will feel when you hear your partner saying, "That shirt looks good on you." When was the last time you heard that? Knowing clearly what you will gain by hitting your goals will be a huge motivator for doing the right things to accomplish them.

The number-one goal-killer is choosing a goal that doesn't match up with your needs, values, and vision—the things you really want. When you set a goal, make sure it's yours and not someone else's. Back in the Corp, I would work hard at meeting my sales goal and winning the annual sales contest, but after winning, I would feel lost and empty inside, almost as if winning was a loss instead of an achievement. I had worked hard and reached my goal, but it wasn't satisfying to me because, the truth is, it was never my goal; it was theirs. And remember what we discussed under attitude in Chapter 11: When you set a goal, you must also believe that you are capable of achieving it. If you don't believe you can do it, you won't. It's as simple as that.

Goal-setting is fundamental to retirement success because it allows us to create the outcomes we want. And goals help us grow, pushing us to feats we could never imagine. For that reason, one of the biggest benefits of setting goals is the person you become while chasing after them. As you hit your objectives, your abilities and your confidence will grow, and you will draw on untapped potential and talents you never knew you had. I still pinch myself every time I get on stage and make a speech. It was all because I set a big goal and had a strong enough "why."

Step 3: Establishing Milestones

For the specific goals and objectives you have identified, you now need to establish some milestones. Milestones are the benchmarks you need to hit in order to make your big goals happen. They allow you to monitor your progress, and without having them in place, chances are high that you will lose momentum and quit pursuing your goal. In my case, for example, a milestone could be hitting a size 38 pair of pants on my way to a 36; or getting an interview with one of the financial planning firms in my area.

Don't forget to celebrate each mini victory. It's important to acknowledge your little wins, the milestones you pass on the way to your big goal. Doing so will actually keep you motivated and make you more likely to accomplish your big vision. When you pass a milestone, you experience a little hit of happiness because you know that you are progressing. As you continue to pass more milestones, your confidence grows; you start to feel like a winner. And when you start feeling like that, there is no stopping you.

Step 4: Always Keeping Your Eye on the Prize

The only thing standing between you and your goal is the bullshit story you keep telling yourself as to why you can't achieve it.

— *Jordan Belfort*

In your daily log, write out the results you want to achieve along with the compelling reason why you want to accomplish that particular goal. List all the actions you intend to track, and every day record your progress toward each goal. It's key to keep track of your progress along the way, as it will inspire you to keep going.

To increase the odds of you hitting your goals, you need to remind yourself of them daily until they are ingrained in your mind.

- Review them each time you write in your daily log at night.
- Put them on your fridge or bathroom mirror.

- Use them as the screen saver on your phone and computer.
- Carry them with you on a 3 x 5 plasticized card in your pocket.

Having your goals pop up throughout your day will remind you of your "whys" and your vision for retirement. Seeing them on a regular basis will help prevent you from slipping and will give you that little extra push to do the things you need to get done to achieve your vision.

Step 5: Creating Your Weekly Schedule

Just because you're retired doesn't mean you don't need some kind of schedule. Sure, freedom and flexibility sound great, but the facts are that many retirees default to living unproductive, unhappy, and unfulfilling retirements, because they are not intentional with their time and don't focus on doing the activities that will give them purpose and meaning and make them truly happy.

> Nobody wrote down a plan to be fat, lazy, or stupid. That's what happens when you don't have a plan.
>
> —Larry Winget

Contrary to what the advertisers keep telling us, it's a big mistake to believe that a retirement based on total leisure will make you happy, because happiness doesn't work that way. Most retirees fall into the trap of thinking that they will be over-the-moon happy when they can spend every day doing something they like and that they couldn't do every day while working. Many retirees have discovered, to their dismay, that doing such things as playing golf every day gets boring really fast. For the record, I found out the same thing holds true for fishing, although it's something I love to do. Variety is the spice of retirement and purpose is what keeps driving us forward. Successful retirees invest their time in many different activities, taking the opportunity to do new, meaningful things and not fall into a rut.

Creating your own weekly schedule will give you back the structure and routine that you lost when you retired and give you back control over how you use your time. It will also make sure that you are making time for the things that are most important to you, and the things you need to do in the short-term to hit your long-term goals. From now on, instead of just drifting, you will know exactly what you are doing, why you are doing it, and when.

Organize your key activities on a daily and weekly basis. You don't have to be busy every minute of the day, you just need to make sure you don't miss doing anything important. Make sure to schedule in what makes you come alive as well as the daily and weekly activities you need to undertake to hit the milestones that will ensure you achieve your long-term goals and objectives.

> Most of the time we feel tired not because we've done too much, but because we've done too little of what makes us come alive.
>
> —Jim Kwik

Make time for practicing your art (whatever that means to you), as well as for exercise activities, volunteer work, going on new adventures, learning how to dance, learning a new language for that trip you have planned, and working, if you have chosen to continue doing that. And above all else, make sure to schedule some time each and every day for doing something you love with people you love.

Get into the habit of planning every day the night before and every week on Sunday. Each Sunday evening, sit down and write out in your journal all the things you want to accomplish the following week. By doing this, you will dramatically increase your chances for retirement success. Each day, after you have finished logging everything in your journal at night, you need to schedule out your next day. Schedule your priorities first; these are your non-negotiables, the important things that you need to get done no matter what—your workouts, elder-care, work, and so on. Once you've made time for them, then you can schedule in your other less important tasks, like cutting the lawn or getting a haircut.

> The key is not to prioritize what's on your schedule, but to schedule your priorities.
> —Stephen Covey

A useful approach is to schedule the hardest thing first, so you tackle it when your mind is clear, and you are at your strongest and most creative. For example, if your immediate priority is to find a job, schedule in time for job searching and networking. After that task is completed, you can move onto something else, like going to the gym.

> If it's your job to eat a frog, it's best to do it first thing in the morning. If it's your job to eat two frogs, it's best to eat the biggest one first.
> —Mark Twain

Here are a couple of scheduling mistakes to watch out for:

Less Is More

A common mistake for many retirement "newbies" is being in a hurry to accomplish everything on your bucket list and trying to do too much in a short space of time. That will only end up making you frustrated and driving you a little crazy, like it did to me. Our goal in retirement is to reduce stress, not create more of it. So, start slow, find your own comfortable pace, and avoid overscheduling yourself by packing too much into a week. I know you are in a hurry to make things better, but Rome wasn't built in a day and neither will be your retirement.

Bracket Creep

Don't let your work or whatever you have identified as your art suffocate your other interests. You need to set boundaries so you can make time for other things that are important to you, and to make sure you stick to those priorities as well. If you allow bracket creep to happen, you will fall behind on your other key goals and may be forced to delay them or possibly give up on them entirely. This is where I got into trouble.

I needed to finish writing my first book, *Victory Lap Retirement*, in order to get my new public speaking and coaching business going. I would get heavy into the writing, and before I knew it, it had consumed most of my day, resulting in me missing out on my workouts and other things as well. Ignoring my other key goals just to get the book done frustrated me and stressed me out.

To create your own version of Retirement Heaven, you need to find balance and the right mix of work, leisure, health, and relationships. Working too much, or focusing on just one thing, throws everything else out of kilter, and it can come back and bite you in the ass hard.

LESSONS FROM A PANDEMIC

Being forced to stay home during the COVID-19 pandemic gave many people a chance to experience what life is like when you don't have to work every day, and some didn't like it at all. After a while, those who couldn't work from home started to go a little stir crazy with all the free time on their hands.

People needed to get back in balance and create a new sense of normalcy. They accomplished this by creating new routines and setting goals for themselves, similar to what we have outlined in this chapter. Putting structure back into their lives enhanced their overall well-being, increased their resiliency, and decreased the chances of them falling into a depression. Creating new schedules and routines and finding new purpose didn't cure the virus, but it mitigated the negative effects of isolation by taking people's minds off it and giving them some control over their daily lives again.

Monitor Your Progress: Evaluate Each Day

It's all well and good to plan your retirement lifestyle carefully, identify your goals clearly, and schedule time for those priorities, but how are you actually doing? The happy ending you are trying to create for the movie of your life will never happen if you don't monitor your progress and check in with how you're doing on your objectives in the short-term.

At the end of every day, take some time to evaluate how you did that day. Have you used your time the way you intended? Did you follow the schedule you set out for yourself? When completing your journal at night, take the time to evaluate the quality of your day:

- Did you get your workouts in?
- Did you eat healthy?
- Did you do some fun things?
- Did you learn or try anything new?
- Did you allow any bad habits to creep back in?
- Did you waste time on useless activities?
- Did you spend some quality time with family and friends?

If I'm attempting to make a habit change such as not eating junk food, I award myself with a gold star in my journal if I toed the line that day. Giving yourself a gold star at the end of the day makes you feel good, and seeing an unbroken series of stars in your journal will motivate you to keep the streak going. Likewise, if you're getting off track and not spending time on the things that are important to you, this daily review will help to keep you honest and to quickly get back on track.

Find Yourself a Couple of Role Models

When it comes to setting clear goals, learn from others who have done what you want to do. Copy how they did it, and you will save yourself a lot of time and speed up your progress. And don't

> If you want to be successful, find someone who has achieved the results you want and copy what they do, and you'll achieve the same results.
>
> —Tony Robbins

be shy about reaching out to them for advice, direction, and encouragement. You will find out like I did that many role models are happy to lend a helping hand.

Learn different things from different role models. You can pick a role model who has been successful at the type of business that you want to start, and you can choose someone else to be a health role model to help you get back into shape. There are so many role models to choose from who have already done what you are trying to do.

And it's not just famous people who serve as good retirement role models. There are plenty of "ordinary" Retirement Rebels around who are doing some great and interesting things. Think about the following:

- Who inspires you?
- What has your role model accomplished that you want to accomplish?
- What qualities does your role model have that you respect?
- What aspects of their lifestyle do you admire?

Just remember that all your role models at some point were afraid just like you feel right now. They had their own doubts about whether what they were attempting would work or not. They were afraid, but they had a strong "why," worked hard, and didn't quit, and because of that look at where they are now. They did it, and so can you.

Create Your Own Adventure Book

It's a good idea to create an adventure book for yourself, a physical expression of what you plan on doing and where you plan on going in the years ahead. A similar idea is to create a vision board—a big collage of pictures and words that represent your hopes and dreams for the future. Personally, I prefer the adventure book myself because it allows more space for a variety of inspiring material. Cut out pictures and stories from the newspaper, magazines, or online sources about what other people have done that you want to do and experience and put them in a binder.

There is nothing better on a cold, snowy day than to browse through your adventure book and see what you have planned for the future; and it's just as satisfying to see what you have already been able to knock off your bucket list. Looking at it will make you smile remembering all the wonderful experiences and fun you had, and it will cause you to start dreaming and looking ahead in anticipation for all the adventures and personal challenges you have planned for the years ahead.

Some examples that you might want to put in your binder could be images representing things like this:

- visiting the Roman Colosseum
- learning to scuba dive
- going fly fishing for trout in Chile
- taking the family to Disney
- joining Toastmasters and giving your first speech
- traveling across Canada on a bicycle
- doing charity work in Africa
- starting a new business/blog
- learning ballroom dancing
- going to cooking school in France

The possibilities are endless, and I could go on listing them forever. What are you dreaming of? What images and stories will you put in your own adventure book?

My Story

I know myself well enough now to realize that not having goals and wasting my time sitting on a couch watching TV being bored out of my mind would kill me before long. Having purpose, meaning, and a sense of achievement are needs of mine that I can't just turn off. I always need something to chase after, to aspire to, and to be better at. To be happy I always need to find another metaphorical mountain to climb. That's just who I am, and I've discovered there are a lot of other retirees just like me who feel the same way. But it took me a while to get to my new "why," the purpose that would drive me in retirement. It evolved gradually in my transition from full-time work to the Victory Lap that I am now living.

My "why" for working in my old bank job was all about providing financial security for my family, and I lost that work "why" when I achieved financial independence and the worry over protecting my family was gone. Losing my "why" caused me to start thinking differently about my job. The bank had changed over the years, I no longer liked working there and needed a change; but as many of you know, it's hard to leave a well-paying job late in your career.

A wake-up call came one day when I tried to buy some extra life insurance. After going through the standard health tests, I was refused coverage because my blood pressure was so high. Seeing the look of concern on the insurance agent's face when he told me the news made me wake up to the fact that I was going to die unless I changed my ways and got healthy. The fear of possibly dying before my time became my new "why" and it is what motivates me to get to the swimming pool when it is –20°C outside. I want to live a long time and enjoy it as much as I can with the Contessa. I want to be around for the kids and make sure they get off to a good start in life. I've developed strong "whys" for each of the nine retirement principles. Those "whys," along with my vision for my future, drives every decision that I make and the actions I take to achieve the goals I've set for myself.

Retirement success is all about having a big vision followed by small steps. At age sixty-five (or older) I'm never going to win an Ironman, but I know that if I show up and train every day, I will finish one. Success comes from showing up, doing the work, returning tomorrow, and doing it again. For me, the working out isn't the hard part; it's the showing up on a regular basis that is tough. There are days when I don't feel like going to the gym or pool, but I know that if I can just make it there, it will be another step in the right direction for me. Following the five-step goal-setting process outlined in this chapter gives me the structure and discipline to follow through on the commitments I've made to myself.

I've made some changes in my lifestyle, including getting rid of some bad habits, which has resulted in some good improvements. I'm sleeping better, I have more energy, I'm writing better (at least it feels like I am) and even better, my blood pressure has dropped by twenty points. What I love about having a weekly schedule is that I wake up each day knowing exactly what I need to do. For me that means:

- Getting up at 4:30 a.m. and working on my book and blog for two hours daily, five days a week.
- Working out six days a week for two hours minimum.

Getting up that early to write allows me to accomplish my most important work first and get it out of the way before I have had my first cup of coffee. This leaves me with the rest of the day for the fun stuff, the stuff that really lights me up. I also focus on scheduling things that will make the Contessa happy, like signing us up for dance lessons at the community center. I'm still sharp enough to know that when the Contessa is happy, I'm happy.

I refuse to do retired-people things like play golf five times a week and go to retired-people luncheons. In fact, I've never been to one, although they keep sending me invitations. I just wouldn't feel comfortable being there because I'm really not retired like the rest of them and it would be hard to relate. Besides, I have too much other fun stuff I would rather do. I enjoy creating goals that stretch me beyond what I have done before. I'm constantly raising the bar, and while it can be uncomfortable and hard, it really feels good when I eventually hit my goals. That's what makes my Victory Lap fun for me.

When you're setting ambitious goals for yourself in retirement, it's important to realize that starting something new usually takes longer than you think, especially if you are unsure what exactly is involved, like starting a retirement coaching business in my case. By putting a specific date on my goal that turned out to be unrealistic, I created a lot of unnecessary pressure for myself and, in hindsight, why did I need to be in such a hurry? I really didn't need the money to live on, and it was a big mistake to put that kind of pressure on myself when it didn't need to happen. Take it from me: be patient, save yourself a lot of stress, and take your time so you can do it right.

Another thing to keep in mind is that not every goal needs to be as ambitious as starting a new business or climbing a mountain. An important goal for you, as it is for me, might be leading a simpler life. I've been working away at trying to make my life less complicated, stripping away at things, and getting rid of stuff. The Contessa and I have gone from room to room in our house, cleaning out all the drawers and closets. I've gotten rid of those pants and shirts that were no longer in style, the ones I would never wear again. Embarrassingly, I even found that some still had tags on them. They no longer fit either, but I couldn't see them because of all the other clothes piled on them. How dumb is that? What a waste of hard-earned money!

I keep trying to slow things down so I can spend more time smelling the roses. I want to spend more time enjoying what I already have, and I plan on spending more time at the cottage, listening to the loons and reading a good book on the dock. I don't recognize my old stressed-out self anymore, and I like that because I never did like that person very much. I'm still working on my Victory Lap, refining it, trying to make it better. I constantly look for ways to add more fun to my days, filling them with interesting and meaningful activities that are aligned with my big-picture goals. One thing I've learned about retirement is to never say never and always to be open to new things.

A good day for me contains some of the things listed below— not all of them in one day, of course (that would kill me!), but one or two of my biggest priorities and favorite activities in various combinations on different days:

- Getting up at 4:30 and working on either my book or a blog article.
- Having coffee, reading the paper, and watching the morning news.
- Having a light breakfast.
- Working out.
- Learning to speak Italian.
- Having lunch with some friends.
- Doing some retirement coaching.
- Learning how to use Instagram and other apps/software.
- Going fishing.
- Hanging out with my tribe.
- Having dinner.
- Going for a walk with the Contessa.

- Giving a presentation.
- Before going to bed, reviewing my to-do list for the next day and updating my daily journal.

A good year looks like a bunch of good days strung together, with some peak events thrown in that could be regular annual events or "specials." I like specials because I enjoy mixing things up and experiencing new things.

An example of a good year would look something like this:

- Fishing trip to the George (annual)
- Taking a trip to Italy (special)
- Going to a bike camp in North Carolina (special)
- Spending a month of the winter in Mexico (annual)
- Participating in the Ironman in Cozumel Mexico (special)

Just writing out these lists made me feel good because I'm in control of my time and finally doing the things that I know will make me happy. While I love my work, I try to restrict it to twenty hours a week so there is ample time to do the other things that I enjoy as well.

Retirement Goals vs. Retirement as "The Goal"

One day I gave a talk to a large group of seniors at a community event. The audience was wrong for me, as they were older seniors set in their ways and they lived a lifestyle that I found, to be blunt, quite boring. Being comfort-oriented retirees, they couldn't really relate to my talk, but they were willing to sit there and listen because they had nothing else better to do with their time. Their happiness levels had plateaued. That was as good as it was going to get, and they were comfortable and willing to accept that. After my presentation, there was a draw, and I was amazed at how excited the group was over the possibility of winning a coffee gift card. It was obviously the highlight of their day, and thinking about this scared me. Living like that gives me nightmares because one of my biggest fears is living a boring, mediocre retirement.

Many retirees view retirement as their ultimate goal, and once they achieve it, they are left with nothing else to shoot for. It will be life as usual, and that is when the boredom sets in. Creating and achieving your own specific goals for living your dreams through-out your retirement will give you the direction that most retirees lack, which eliminates uncertainty, stress, and boredom. Because of that, you will be more productive and more fulfilled than retir-ees who continue to just drift and accept things as they are.

My advice to you is never be satisfied: keep stretching, ex-ploring, learning, and experiencing. Create a bucket list a mile long and keep knocking things off that list as long as you can, and when you achieve them, keep making new ones. You will find like I did that what lies on the other side of your goals is Retirement Heaven—the Victory Lap of your dreams.

While there were a few bumps early on, Mike was confident that his movie would have a good ending.

Questions for Self-Reflection

- What does retirement success mean to you?
- What does your ideal retirement look like?
- What do you want your retirement life to look like in five years and in ten years with respect to relationships, health, work, purpose, and growth?
- What would a good day look like to you? What would a good year look like?
- Where do you want to invest your time, energy, and money?
- Are you doing the best you can? Can you do better?
- What is holding you back?
- What do you have to lose if you just go for it?
- If you had all the money you need, how would you live your life differently?
- Do you have purposeful goals?
- Which of your goals satisfies your needs and values?
- What outcomes do you expect from your goals?
- How will hitting your goals improve the quality of your retirement?
- How will hitting each of your goals make you feel?
- What pain would you feel from not achieving your goals, and what pleasure would you experience from achieving them?
- How will hitting your goals change you?
- What goals are on your bucket list?
- If you were living your ideal retirement, what would you be doing every day/week/month/year?

Simple Truths

- You're the director of your own life story. The sooner you decide to have a better script, the sooner you get to live a more awesome retirement.
- The quality of your retirement is the difference between your positive habits and your negative habits.
- To be successful, you need a compelling "why" for doing what you're doing.
- You can rely on willpower to get you to the gym, but it's your "why" that gets you to stay there and do the required workouts.

- It's not what you do; it's why you do it that makes the difference.
- If it doesn't challenge you, it won't change you.
- Comfort and leisure are great, but they are not enough for a fulfilling retirement.
- A well-designed retirement lifestyle is generative; it is constantly creative, productive, changing, and evolving.
- Retirement is good when you can get up in the morning and know that what you are going to do still matters.
- In Victory Lap, fulfillment comes from designing your own life.
- The one thing you can focus on and improve on is you.
- Goal-setting is the most effective way of achieving your dreams.
- The ultimate goal in Victory Lap is to become the best version of you possible.
- If you schedule more of the positives, there will be less room for any negatives.
- Following in the footsteps of others who have done what you want to do will put you on the fast track to success.
- Setting big goals so you can continue to grow is hard, and that is why so few retirees choose to do it. But if you want to enjoy an awesome retirement, that's the price of admission.

18

Retirement—Heaven or Hell?

The Choice Is Yours

Heaven and hell is right now. . . . You make it heaven or you make it hell by your actions.
—George Harrison

As we said back in Chapter 1, retirement feels great during the honeymoon stage. There is nowhere to be, no deadlines, no stress, and no pressure to perform. But after a while, for many of us, what at first seemed like freedom reveals itself as a new form of hell.

There is an old *Twilight Zone* episode called "A Nice Place to Visit" that brings this point home. In it, the main character is Rocky Valentine, a small-time thief who is shot during a robbery and loses consciousness. He wakes up and at some point he realizes that he's in fact dead, but by some mistake instead of being in hell where he belongs, he's in heaven and has been assigned a guardian angel by the name of Mr. Pip. Life for Rocky is great for a while, as all his wishes are catered to: there are beautiful women, fancy clothes, an expensive penthouse, and all the money he desires. In fact, every time he goes to the casino, no matter what game he plays he wins; he can't lose. But eventually Rocky gets bored of the predictability of his life; the excitement is gone, and with it, all of the fun too. Finally, Rocky can't take it any longer and pleads with Mr. Pip to send him to the other place where he belongs and says that he doesn't deserve to be in heaven. At this point Mr. Pip replies, "Whatever gave you the idea that you were in heaven? This is the other place!"

The lesson here is that Rocky goes crazy because he is trapped in a boring, predictable, meaningless life. There are no challenges, there is no effort required on his part, and there's nothing to look forward to because it all exists as soon as he wants it. Sounds a little bit like those retirement commercials the advertisers like to keep showing us, doesn't it?

We've been conditioned by society to think of retirement as the payoff for all our hard work; a life of endless leisure where everyone lives happily ever after. But the reality is that, just like in the *Twilight Zone* episode, any retirement based solely on leisure— for example, sitting on a beach somewhere drinking Margaritas all day—usually ends in boredom, and boredom is a living hell. There is only so much reading, watching TV, shopping, traveling, and visiting friends a person can handle before they start feeling like Rocky did and thinking that maybe it would be more fun in the other place.

Many people go through hell when they retire, including those with a lot of money. They are embarrassed and frustrated about feeling like that because they have been told that this will be the best time of their lives and they can't understand why they're so miserable and unfulfilled. In order to be happy

Retirement Heaven is filled with the sound of beautiful music.
Retirement Hell, not so much.

in retirement we need to be constantly challenged, and not just by who hits the longest drive. It's about finding a suitable way to satisfy our innate needs and our true mission in life, and until we find a way to do that, retirement is not going to be a lot of fun. That's just the way it is.

Retirement Hell

Some of us will spend some time in Retirement Hell until we figure things out and discover our answer for what we need to do next.

Retirement Hell is boring as hell (pun intended) and your most important conversation there, which gets repeated numerous times throughout the day, is about what the weather forecast is or what you are going to eat. Small talk is painful and exhausting, and it will kill both your soul as well as the soul of the person who you are talking to. It's a classic lose-lose scenario.

> A perpetual holiday is a good working definition of hell.
>
> —George Bernard Shaw

Retirement Hell is a place for nonbelievers: for people who don't believe in planning and goal-setting, for people who made bad choices, and for people who didn't make any choices at all. It's a place filled with your fears. The devil knows what scares you and just keeps these fears in your face and laughs at how they stop you from taking any steps forward.

And it's not just boredom and fear that you need to be concerned with. Retirement Hell comes in many forms:

- After working long hours for so many years to take care of your family, now that you do have the time, they don't want to be near you.
- Getting divorced late in life.
- Living with someone you don't like and who doesn't like you, for the rest of your life.
- Your TV is your best and only friend.
- Living with regret.
- Being forced to do bad work—work that you hate doing— just because you need the money.
- Living on a fixed income and feeling that your world is shrinking a little bit each year.
- Having nightmares every night about your old job and how they threw you out, and not being able to move forward.
- Not being able to sleep at night because you're worried that you might live too long and run out of retirement savings.
- Discovering that you have a debilitating illness and there is a cure for it, but you can't afford to pay for it.
- Having lots of money but not being physically able to get out of bed in the morning and do the things that you want to spend the money on.
- Spending the next thirty years of life not having a reason to get out of bed in the morning, instead just killing time watching TV and waiting for the Grim Reaper to come.

- Losing your health along with your independence and being forced to live in a nursing home.
- Having no friends and living a meaningless life.

Beware the Black Swan

And it's not just bad choices or lack of planning that could cause you to fall into Retirement Hell. You could be hit out of the blue by a "black swan" event, something that is unexpected and has a major effect on your retirement. You can't predict or defend against black swan events—they just happen when they happen—but you still end up in Retirement Hell because of them through no fault of your own.

Examples of black swan events:

- Having the most important person in your life (your spouse or partner) die unexpectedly soon after you both retire.
- Soon after retiring, learning that there is a problem with your company pension and that they plan on cutting your benefits by 50 percent.
- Doing all the right things for your health and still being struck with terminal cancer.
- Watching your retirement savings vaporize during a global pandemic or some other kind of severe market downturn.

It's because of the possibility of black swan events that we urge retirees not to defer happiness like we used to do during our working years, and instead to enjoy each and every day to the fullest. You just never know what might happen.

> . . . you never know how soon it will be too late.
> —Ralph Waldo Emerson

LESSONS FROM A PANDEMIC

For people of a certain age, the COVID-19 pandemic was a dress rehearsal for retirement and gave them a feel for how different life will be when they stop working full-time.

What had previously been just an academic thought for people considering packing it in suddenly turned into reality, and many discovered they were not ready for retirement or decided that traditional retirement was not for them. They didn't know what to do with all the free time on their hands. They didn't have much in the way of hobbies and purpose, and those deficiencies were amplified during the lockdown. The pandemic taught these folks that they need to get better prepared than they are for life after work.

The pandemic scared us and opened our eyes to the reality of how empty and purposeless life can be when we don't (or can't) plan for it. We need to use that fear to motivate us to prepare properly for whatever route we choose to take.

Escaping Retirement Hell

If you want things to be different, perhaps the answer is to become different yourself.

—*Norman Vincent Peale*

The good news is that after reading this book, you now know how to escape from that godforsaken place or avoid it altogether and how to become healthy and happy again. All you need to do is become a Retirement Rebel and start doing the right things for *you*, and before you know it, you will be in that other, better place—the place you deserve to be. Self-awareness is the way out of Retirement Hell. Many of us cannot handle uncomfortable self-examination, but until we do that, we will remain stuck there.

Follow the nine retirement principles and reduce stress in your life by exercising, eating right, and finding purpose. Be social, join tribes, and make a lot of friends. Make it a priority to spend most of your time with people you care about and who care about you. Be an adventurer and live outside your comfort zone, exploring, learning, and doing interesting and exciting things. By becoming a Retirement Rebel, you finally have a chance to unleash your passion and creativity—parts of yourself that you may have kept bottled up inside for years. All you have to do now is choose to go after it instead of just sitting on the couch in Retirement Hell and moaning for the rest of your life.

Retirement Heaven

Retirement Heaven is where the smart retirees end up. There is no more hiding or pretending—all the phoniness has been stripped away and all that remains is the real you. It's where you connect with your inner child again, returning to that special place where anything is possible and there is always another adventure to go on. Unlike Retirement Hell, in Retirement Heaven we have enough money to do the things we want to do, along with good health, strong relationships with family and friends, and fun recreational interests including work and other things that stimulate us and get us excited to jump out of bed every morning.

Retirement Heaven is all about happiness and freedom. It's a beautiful sunrise, the laughter of a grandchild, a fish on the end of a line. It's about living in the moment and not being stressed out over what tomorrow might bring. It's about freedom of choice and the freedom of time to be spontaneous and do things on the spur of the moment. The freedom to travel, the freedom to follow your passions and submerge yourself in your art, whatever that may be. Most important, it's about being intentional about what you do, how you spend your time, and who you spend it with. No one is ever bored or lonely in Retirement Heaven, and that is a true blessing.

Understand What Retirement Happiness Really Is

The three components of happiness are something to do, someone to love, and something to look forward to.

—Gordon Livingston

Retirement happiness is an attitude; it's action; it's activity with purpose. It's about filling your day with interesting, meaningful activities and hitting your values on a regular basis. It's about being generous and finding ways to give back to the community and helping people in need. It's about growing and evolving, trying, and learning something new. It's about challenging yourself—attempting something that is not easy, that taxes you, that stretches you, that allows you to realize your potential a little more each day. Happiness is in the struggle of getting there. It's about being tested and proving worthy. It can be in the form of participating in an athletic event, practicing your art, or simply volunteering for a good cause. Retirement happiness is being able to always find another mountain to climb. It's hard to be disappointed about retirement when you are busy doing interesting, fun, purposeful things.

The paradox about Retirement Heaven is that you are never really completely retired, and the process of becoming never stops until the very end. In Retirement Heaven there are no limits to what you can aspire to do, and you are always busy doing something, but it's a good, fun kind of busy. You go from doing things that you have to do, to doing things that you want to do, and this makes all the difference in the world.

In Retirement Heaven:

- The only schedule you follow is your schedule.
- The dress code is casual and you can wear whatever you want.
- The stress is gone—you are free from work pressures: the pressure to perform, the bad bosses, the deadlines, the always-growing sales goals, and the competition. The endless pursuit of status, power, and wealth is finally over. Hallelujah!
- Because the stress is gone, you sleep better. And if you feel tired, you can take a nap whenever you want.
- Your family relationships are better than ever because you have more time to spend with them and the pressure is off. More time, for example, to go for a walk with your spouse or to a music concert with the kids.
- You replace your work ethic with an enjoyment ethic. Work is optional in Retirement Heaven; it's a personal preference.
- You will be in the best physical shape of your life. You now have the time to work out and eat right, and so you will feel better than when you were working full-time.
- There is always another adventure to go on. You can take up a new hobby or take an existing one to the next level. You can go back to school and learn more about subjects you're interested in. You can finish that degree or learn how to paint or play the guitar and fill your days practicing.
- You remain relevant and continue to contribute, and this makes you happy because you know you matter.
- You become who you really are and get to do what you were meant to do—to complete your mission.

My Story

My Victory Lap gives me the freedom and the time to pursue my dreams; the time to develop new interests and find skills that I didn't know I had. My main focus now is to cram as much living into my Victory Lap as I can.

In Victory Lap you are not retiring from life, you are entering a new phase of life where you don't have to focus all your energies on just making a living. A lot of people will choose to go back to work after retiring, but in a new job, a new role, with a new attitude, and much more flexibility. The key is to keep growing and stay engaged.

Today I'm not perfect but I feel good on the inside, and that is what really matters. My life now is better than good because I am not passive about it and I have high expectations for it. That's why I'm excited to get out of bed every morning, and believe me, it's been a long time since I last felt like that.

These days I'm always on the go traveling to places of interest searching for the truth about retirement. I love talking to the Retirement Rebels who attend our seminars and learning about the wonderful fulfilling lifestyles they have created for themselves and then sharing their stories with others so they may learn what is possible.

Personally, I never plan to stop working because, for me, working means thinking, talking, connecting, and creating. Working is my fun, so why would I ever retire from something I love to do? I'm back in that scary and fun place again: living on the edge, way outside my comfort zone; being an explorer; and going on a lot of new adventures. I still have a lot to learn about, and that is what makes retirement interesting and fun for me.

I like to test myself regularly to remind myself what I am capable of. It's turned into a game for me, chasing after the fears that used to control me for most of my life. Now I'm doing presentations in front of large groups of people, preparing to attempt an Ironman Triathlon, and planning on getting into a shark cage and having a close encounter with a great white—things that once would have scared the crap out of me. In Victory Lap, the scary things are the things worth doing.

I'm sleeping better because of the working out and my decision to eat healthier, plus the stress is gone as well. Now when I get up in the morning, I'm excited about the day because I'm doing things that I want to do and that makes a big difference. Today I'm a whole different person and have turned back into that lively and funny guy, the man that I used to be. I'm now at a point where all the pieces in my Victory Lap have finally come together, and I'm finally living the life I always wanted.

I believe I can make a difference, and when I think about it, I spent the last four decades of my life getting ready for this. My Victory Lap is all about giving, not getting. Helping people is a big value of mine, and my work delivers that to me in spades. I love teaching people how to spread their wings again and giving them inspiration and hope. I want them to demand

> We make a living by what we get; we make a life by what we give.
> —Winston Churchill

more out of retirement, to envision more, to learn more, and to become more than they ever imagined. I view my work as my way of giving back, and it's become both my purpose and passion. Believe me, there is nothing sweeter in Victory Lap than to be appreciated for helping others. It always feels good to do good.

Since learning that the effects of aging are reversible, I've been working hard at following the nine retirement principles to improve the odds of living a long, healthy, prosperous life. But I also keep reminding myself that retirement is not a contest about who lives the longest; it's all about reaching your retirement potential and living the best retirement life possible.

I don't want to play small in my retirement. I don't want to squander any of my precious time, and that is why I have a well-thought-out vision for my retirement. I know exactly where I want to be in the next one, three, and five years, and I have established yearly goals that will both help me get there and ensure that I'm having fun every step of the way. Now all I have to do is show up consistently and do the work.

I learned an important lesson about retirement from my mother during my visits with her at the nursing home. At that point, all her possessions were gone, and all she was left with were some pictures and the memories she had accumulated over the years. We spent a lot of time and had a lot of fun talking about all the things she had done and seen over the years and all the special relationships she had developed along the way.

Mike loved telling the grandkids about all the adventures he went on with the Contessa.

People in my mother's situation spend a lot of time reflecting on their life, wondering if they really lived; wondering if they did the best for their children; wondering if they mattered. Watching her go through that taught me that you need to live your life well now, so that when it comes time to ask yourself the same questions, you will be happy with the answers. When it's my time, I want to have a lot of good memories to look back upon and share with my kids and grandkids, like she did. I don't want to have any regrets and lie there wondering "What if?" That would truly be hell!

Everybody Dies, but Not Everybody Lives

It is not death most people are afraid of. It is getting to the end of life, only to realize that you never truly lived.

—Prince Ea

If we have done our job right, after reading this book you should be thinking about your retirement future differently. You should be thinking about retirement not as the ultimate goal, the finish line after all those years of working, but as a new beginning—your chance at a happy, healthy, fulfilling Victory Lap. You shouldn't be scared anymore, and instead you should be excited about life, where you want to take it, and what you plan on getting out of it.

Your retirement success is in your own hands. By now you know what you need to do to create an awesome Victory Lap for yourself, but you can't change things for the better just by reading a book. Just knowing isn't enough—without taking action, it won't happen. Stress comes from learning what you need to do and then not doing it. Your gut will keep telling you to take action; and until you do, the stress will not go away.

> Vision without action is hallucination.
>
> —Thomas Edison

Lots of people know how to lose weight, but they fail because they are unwilling to change their habits and do the required work. Refuse to be like them—take action now on your new knowledge before it's too late. Only applied knowledge will get you on the retirement trajectory you want, so do yourself a favor and start today, not tomorrow. Your retirement choices and actions over the next five to ten years will determine whether you look back upon your retirement with regret or satisfaction.

Getting healthy takes time. Repairing relationships takes time. Making new friends takes time. Starting a new business (especially one that you have never tried before) takes years of hard work, but the payoff in terms of happiness, accomplishment, and satisfaction is huge. Bottom line: the sooner you start, the sooner you will get the retirement outcome you want.

If you are still struggling and having trouble starting, it's smart to ask for help in the form of a good retirement coach. They will save you a lot of time and aggravation and will hold you accountable. They will ensure that you continue to take the small steps even when you don't feel like it, and by doing that, one day you will get there.

You have the power to change the trajectory of your retirement. Why settle for a mediocre retirement and follow along like everyone else when you are capable of so much more? Settling won't make you happy, and you will end up spending the rest of your life wondering, "What if?" At this stage in our lives, we can no longer complain about a lack of time or money. All our past excuses are gone about why we can't just finally go for it and take a swing for the fences. It's your turn! You can live a boring, safe retirement, or you can make a truly remarkable one. The choice is yours. So, what are you waiting for?

Questions for Self-Reflection

- How would you describe your new vision of retirement to a stranger?
- Are you living up to your retirement potential?
- Are you growing, shrinking, or hiding?
- Are you doing what you love?
- What do you want to do/accomplish before you die?

Simple Truths

- If you think retirement is the end goal and expect that simply retiring will solve all your problems, you are in for a rude awakening.
- Some of your best years are still ahead of you.
- You don't want to spend every day in retirement feeling like a victim.
- It's better to wear out than rust out.
- Your action, or lack of action, is the only thing separating you from where you are and where you want to be.
- How can any of us know what we are capable of if we have never tried?
- If you start today and take action to improve things, what comes later will be much better.
- It's never too late to be a beginner and try something new.
- Things get done by doing them. The only thing holding you back from enjoying an awesome Victory Lap is you.
- You will have the retirement that you are willing to put up with.
- The only person to blame if you're not happy with your retirement is the person whose face you see in the mirror every morning.
- Happiness isn't a place at which we arrive, it is an ongoing process.

Acknowledgments

This book was hard to write and on more than one occasion I was ready to throw in the towel and quit. Thankfully, a lot of people came to my rescue and gave me their time and the support and guidance I needed to carry on to the end. I owe them a lot.

Special thanks to: Pat Mason, Ernie Zelinski, Seth Godin, Susan Williams, Rob Morrison, Michelle Oram, Mark Venning, Chris Crowley, Simon Chan, Gerry O'Toole, Bob Lowry, Don Ezra, Jonathan Chevreau, Wealthy Doc, Daryl Diamond, Fritz Gilbert, Steve Nease, Rob Dawson, Lindsay Humphreys and, last but not least, Karen Milner, my editor.

Order the Book That Started It All
Victory Lap Retirement

Our Gift to You

We realize that transitioning to retirement can be a challenging time. Having been through it ourselves, we know that you can lose lots of precious prime retirement time as you try to figure things out by yourself. We would like to help you avoid this.

After reading this book, if you have any questions about anything that we have written, feel free to send an email to us at **victorylapretirement@gmail.com** and we will try to clarify. It's the least we can do for another Retirement Rebel.

Also, be sure to check out what we share over at Booming Encore (www.boomingencore.com). From a retirement advice column to help you transition to retirement, to stories and articles to inform and inspire you, we are here to help. After all, we are all in this together!

To Investment Advisors and Financial Planners

The purpose of this book is to connect the dots between your clients' financial plans and the meaningful, fulfilling retirement they dream of living. After reading it, they will have a good handle on how they wish to spend their next thirty years, which will make your job of turning their dream into reality a whole lot easier.

Instead of giving your clients another coffee cup this year, why not give them the gift of our retirement books instead? Giving them to your clients three to five years before they retire will motivate them to start thinking about their retirement goals, and give both of you lots to talk about as you go through the planning process together.

You can purchase bulk orders at a discount by contacting Mike at **michael.drak@yahoo.ca.**

About the Authors

Michael Drak is a forty-year veteran of the financial services industry and lives with his wife, Melina (also affectionately known as "The Contessa"), in Toronto. He started his Victory Lap Retirement in 2014 and is busy helping others transition into their own personal versions. In addition to mentoring others, he gives speeches and seminars to groups across the country and cultivates and maintains the Victory Lap community at www.victorylapretirement.com.

Susan Williams is founder of Booming Encore (www.boomingencore.com), a digital media hub dedicated to providing information and inspiration to help baby boomers create and live their best life. Prior to launching Booming Encore in 2013, Susan spent twenty-eight years in senior leadership positions in a number of corporations. Today Booming Encore is ranked as a global authority and social media influencer for baby boomers, aging, and retirement as well as being one of the top websites for baby boomers worldwide. Married and living in Montreal, Susan loves to discover ways to live life to the fullest and shares her experiences, observations, and opinions as she lives her own best booming encore.

Robert Morrison, CFP,® is a CERTIFIED FINANCIAL PLANNER™ professional and Chief Strategy and Innovation Officer at Savant Wealth Management in Lincolnshire, Illinois. A wealth advisor for nearly twenty years, Rob is passionate about helping clients navigate the changing retirement landscape and has coached many through their Victory Lap transitions. He has been profiled in *The Wall Street Journal* online and appears regularly in the financial media, including Morningstar.com. Rob is actively engaged in the Victory Lap community at www.victorylapretirement.com.